BLOOD AND TEARS
Perspectives on Conflict

About the Editors

Badakynti Nylla Iangngap serves as an Assistant Professor, Department of English, Synod College, Shillong. She is currently pursuing her Ph.D. entitled "Representation of Self: A Select Study of Literary Texts by Khasi Writers and Transcribers" from the Department of English, North-Eastern Hill University. She completed her M.Phil. entitled "Stalemated Narratives: Reconsidering the Historical and the Literary in the Khasi Context" from Department of English, University of Delhi.

Dr. Mankhrawbor Dunai currently serves as an Assistant Professor at Synod College, Shillong. He was awarded his Ph.D. for his work entitled "Children's Literature and the Adult Encounter: A Critical Study of C.S. Lewis's The Chronicles of Narnia Series" from the Department of English, North-Eastern Hill University. He was also a recipient of the Rajiv Gandhi National Fellowship Award and was a Senior Research Fellow during his Ph.D. research.

Dr. Gayreen Lyngdoh serves as an Associate Professor, Department of English, Synod College, Shillong. Her M.Phil. thesis was on "The crisis of identity in Langston Hughes' Poetry" while her doctoral thesis was on "The Journey to the Self: A Study of the Women Characters in Select Novels of Pearl S. Buck and Amy Tan."

BLOOD AND TEARS
Perspectives on Conflict

Edited by

Badakynti Nylla Iangngap
Mankhrawbor Dunai
Gayreen Lyngdoh

CONCEPT PUBLISHING COMPANY PVT. LTD.
NEW DELHI - 110 059

ISBN: 978-93-5594-631-7

First Published 2023

Published and Printed by

Concept Since 1974

Concept Publishing Company Pvt. Ltd.
A/15-16, Commercial Block, Mohan Garden
New Delhi-110059 (India)
T: +91-11-41101460
E: publishing@conceptpub.com, *W*: www.conceptpub.com

Cataloging in Publication--Courtesy: D.K. Agencies (P) Ltd. <docinfo@dkagencies.com>

Eye for an Eye: Conflict in South Asia (Seminar) (2019 : Shillong, India)
Blood and tears : perspectives on conflict / edited by Badakynti Nylla Langngap, Mankhrawbor Dunai, Gayreen Lyngdoh.
pages cm
Papers presented at an international seminar on the theme "Eye for an Eye: Conflict in South East Asia", organised by Department of English, Synod College during November 6-7, 2019.
Includes bibliographical references and index.
ISBN 9789355946317

1. Social conflict--South Asia--Congresses. 2. Social conflict--India, Northeastern--Congresses. 3. Ethnic conflict--South Asia--Congresses. 4. Ethnic conflict--India, North eastern--Congresses. I. Langngap, Badakynti Nylla, editor. II. Dunai, Mankhrawbor, editor. III. Lyngdoh, Gayreen, editor. IV. Synod College (Shillong, India). Department of English, organizer. V. Title.

LCC HN687.E94 2019 | DDC 303.60954 23

Acknowledgements

In the beginning of 2019, the Department of English, Synod College initiated a discussion on the need and desirability of having a platform whereby scholars and academicians, social scientists and activists, artists and policy-makers, could come together to discourse and debate on issues that are interdisciplinary and of cross-cutting relevance both in academia and society at large. These discussions culminated in an International Seminar on the theme "Eye for an Eye: Conflict in South East Asia". The thought-provoking papers and robust discussions generated in the seminar, covering a broad canvas stretching from the South East Asia platform to the national, regional and local arena, were so compelling that a need was felt to compile these in book form. Hence, this book! As we publish this, we want to acknowledge all those whose suggestions, advice and contribution, literary and otherwise, have helped in bringing out this book.

The Department of English, Synod College for taking the initiative and for the teamwork involved; the Principal of the College, Dr R.M. Lyngdoh for his support and encouragement; Dr M.Rani, the then Coordinator of IQAC and currently the Vice Principal, for giving us the nudge in the conduct of the seminar and subsequent publishing of the outcome; the many helpers on and behind the scene; above all, the seminar participants and paper contributors whose scholarship and academic inputs have resulted in this book. We hope that it will serve as a significant resource and knowledge pool in future scholastic endeavours and research. Thank You and God bless!

Editors

List of Contributors

Batriti Nongbri, Assistant Professor, Department of Environmental Science, Shillong College.

Bennathaniel H. Diengdoh, Assistant Professor, Department of Environmental Science, Shillong College.
Email: diengdoh.benc87@gmail.com

Cr Patricia Mary Hodge, PhD Research Scholar, Department of English, North-Eastern Hill University. **Email:** patclhodge93@gmail.com

Dixita Deka, PhD Research Scholar, Tata Institute of Social Sciences (TISS), Guwahati Campus, Assam.
Email: guwahatidixita719@gmail.com

Fakrul Alam (Prof.), Department of English, University of Dhaka.
Email: falam1951@du.ac.bd

Harshana Rambukwella (Prof.), Director, Post-Graduate Institute of English (PGIE), Open University of Sri Lanka.
Email : h.rambukwella@gmail.com

Kaveri Khound, PhD Research Scholar, North-Eastern Hill University, Shillong, Meghalaya, **Email:** kaverikhound100@gmail.com

Kethoser (Aniu) Kevichusa : **Email:** aniu@rzimindia.in

Laiamon Naomi Nengnong, Assistant Professor, Synod College, Shillong.
Email: laiamonnengnong@gmail.com

Lede E, Miki Pohshna, PhD Research Scholar, Department of English, North-Eastern Hill University. **Email:** ledeemiki@gmail.com

Ruth Ibameri Kharbamon, Assistant Professor, Sankardev College, Shillong. **Email:** ruthkharbamon.08@gmail.com

Sukalpa Bhattacharjee (Prof.), Department of English, North-Eastern Hill University, Shillong. **Email:** bsukalpa@hotmail.com

Tiewri Lyngdoh-Nonglait, Assistant Professor, Department of Environmental Science, Shillong College.

Contents

Acknowedgements v
List of Contributors vi
Introduction ix

Section I

1. Terror, Affect and Literary Representation : Reflections on Sri Lankan Writing in a South Asian Frame 3
– *Harshana Rambukwella*

2. Confronting Violence Relating to National Identity Formation : A Bangladeshi Perspective 15
– *Fakrul Alam*

3. Imagery and Reality : Art from the Rohingyas 33
– *Laiamon Naomi Nengnong*

Section II

4. Gender and Conflict 47
–*Sukalpa Bhattacharjee*

5. Re-Imagining the Catholic Imagination: Queer, Self and Conflict in Norman E. Pasaribu's *Sergius Seeks Bacchus* 59
– *Lede-e-miki Pohshna*

6. Skin Colour Hierarchy:The Ideal Filipina Beauty and the Conflict of Colour 73
– *Cr Patricia Mary Hodge*

Section III

7. A Study of the Relationship between Environmental Change, Migration and Conflict : The South-South-east Asian Scenario 87
– Bennathaniel H. Diengdoh, Batriti Nongbri and *Tiewri Lyngdoh-Nonglait*

8. Impact of Ethnic Conflict on Agriculture and Sustainable Rural Development in Bodoland Territorial Area District (BTAD) in Assam 102
– Kaveri Khound

Section IV

9. The Naga Story of Conflict 113
–Kethoser (Aniu) Kevichusa

10. The Khasi Indigenous Beliefs and Christianity: An Encounter or a Negotiation? 127
– Ruth Ibameri Kharbamon

11. Rumours, Suspicions, and the Making of the Narrative: Remembering the *Secret Killings* in Assam 137
– Dixita Deka

Index 149

Introduction

Conflict has been a constant phenomenon within human societies. It is usually driven by the competition for resources which then spills over into varying arenas be it the socio-political, economic or environmental spheres. Conflicts have shaped and will continue to shape the history of the world. Recent trends in conflict narratives have shown that the idealised notion of a globalised community that must coexist and thrive together is being challenged by the rise of fundamentalism that is being fuelled by increasingly aggressive left as well as right-wing ideologies with each attempting to assert its veracity over the other. Such conflicts that spill from ideological ruptures manifests itself into violence in its various forms be it physical or non-physical in nature with its most extreme form being war. The social, the cultural and the political arenas continue to stir up conditions of instability and conflict that threaten modern society even today. As pointed out by Michael Ray, Francis Fukuyama's thesis of 'the end of history' seems to be challenged with the recent trends of conflict in the 21st century beginning with September 11, 2001, terror attacks. The wars that were the aftermath of September 11, 2001, have only exposed the price of maintaining Western liberal democracy. The rise of capitalism, an obvious offshoot of liberalism has accelerated progress and development at a global scale. But along with such rapid human progress is the ecological imbalance that is at the brink of a spill over. Despite the efforts that have been made by the global scientific community to improve the environmental impact of human activities, there seems to be little improvement and the ecological threat and conflicts that accompany it is a reality we now have to face.

Furthermore, while Fukuyama took into account the conflicting political ideologies that existed, he failed to look at ideologies surrounding identity politics that plague the 21st century. The most recent war between Russia and Ukraine bears testimony to this, for apart from the ideological and geopolitical conflict is also the issue of identity politics. What becomes obvious is that the ramifications of ideological conflict continue to multiply as each facet of humanity is explored. Apart from political ideologies, conflicting religious ideologies seem to be on the rise and are usually branded along with identity politics. The nexus of religion and identity is a dangerous combination, the logical product of which is extremism and fundamentalism, neither of which are conducive to peace or progress. Religious fundamentalism has badly affected politics worldwide and has in turn affected policies at best or has resulted in physical conflict, at worst. What becomes ominous then is that the progress of humanity does not seem to head towards any form of rationality. While influenced by the Hegelian trajectory of human history that has at its end ultimate recognition, Fukuyama also seems to question the ultimate goal of humanity:

> Indeed, does not the desire for unequal recognition constitute the basis of a livable life, not just for bygone aristocratic societies, but also in modern liberal democracies? Will not their future survival depend, to some extent, on the degree to which their citizens seek to be recognised not just as equal, but as superior to others? And might not the fear of becoming contemptible "last men" not lead men to assert themselves in new and unforeseen ways, even to the point of becoming once again bestial "first men" engaged in bloody prestige battles, this time with modern weapons? (Fukuyama, xxiii)

Fukuyama's words are prophetic given our present historical context which is riddled with conflicts arising out of bigoted minds indoctrinated by some ideology or the other. All of this has only aggravated existing social and cultural conflicts, with man as the central agent who plays the dual role of both initiating conflicts as well as making attempts to resolve them. Racism, sexism, religious conflicts, immigration, ecological instability, global political tension, but also at the most basic level of the loss of the physical and mental entity of a home are a few pertinent issues of conflict that are being faced by communities around the world. Such problems are important issues of conflict studies as they take on consequential manifestations of violence, poverty, homelessness, statelessness, degradation of mental and social well-being and eventually affect international relations, global economics and foreign policies.

Despite the criticism faced from many quaters, Johan Galtung's conflict triangle (A: Attitude, B: Behaviour, C: Contradiction) has greatly contributed to our understanding of conflict and its analysis as well as a means in providing conflict resolution. Galtung points out that people's internal attitude (prejudices, beliefs, feelings) towards a situation is largely responsible for situations of conflict, the attitude in turn affects the behaviour of people that can, in turn, aggravate the situation of conflict, and it is this behaviour that manifests itself in some form of conflict. In order to understand and eventually transform/resolve such situations of conflict, we need to keep in mind the contradiction under which such attitudes and behaviour towards the situation of conflict have developed. This method has been widely used in conflict studies. When we look at South-East Asia, the conflicts that have taken place between countries and even ethnic communities within countries show that conflict is still very much a phenomenon that is no closer to being resolved. The notion of aggressive nationalism, the need to preserve the ethnic and cultural identity of a people, not only at the level of discourse but at the ground level as well. These issues have contributed to much of the violence we have witnessed so far and even shows potentialities for future conflict scenarios. Many of these situations of conflict can be studied under the lens of Gultang's triangle theory. A good example of its application is seen in Ionut, Stalenoi's "The People's War" and Johan Galtung's "Conflict Models" in which he applies this theory to the Civil War in Nepal (1996-2006) to study it as a situation of asymmetric conflict. Stalenoi further uses Galtung's triangle of violence (cultural violence, direct violence, structured violence) which serves to show the different forms that violence can take on in situations of conflict as well as map out the means by which such violence can be resolved using the triangle of conflict. Such theories of conflict are especially relevant to keep in mind in the context of this book. And while peace studies have not been touched upon in this book, Gultang's peace theory is also as important to keep in mind in the context of reading, understanding and analysing conflict.

Contextualising our area of study to South Asia/South-East Asia, this book looks at the different aspects of conflict, i.e. gender, racial, ethnic, religious, ecological, ideological, which would fall under Galtung's category of attitude, as well as spill over from such attitudes towards race, gender, identity, ecology etc. that are a result of the manifesting behaviour of society. Contributors to this book have been able to bring about a more nuanced understanding of representing conflict/violence, living it, understanding it, narrativizing it and analysing its effects on society. Harshana Rambukwella talks about his personal encounters with violence and terror in Sri Lanka during the 1900s and early 2000s and takes into account how violence is narrativised in literature and also represented by selected Sri Lankan writers. He also contextualises this representation within the post-colonial framework to examine the colonial baggage that is almost always taken as part of the post-colony without questioning as well as the problems of the nation state within the post-colonial context. Rambukwella especially questions the represenation of terror that feeds on the global discourse on terror that has gained momentum from the 9/11 attack on U.S.A. that can in turn be detrimental especially for Third World countries of South Asia.

In his paper, "Confronting Violence relating to National Identity Formation – A Bangladeshi Perspective", Fakrul Alam like Rambukwella, draws on his personal experiencee and history, to talk about how in Bangladesh, a nation which has had to contend with three "partitions" in less than a century, conflict and violence were inevitably linked to the politics of identity, an identity forged primarily by religion and language—the religion being Muslim, the language being Bengali. Building on Amartya Sen's work, *Identity and Violence: The Illusion of Destiny*, Alam argues how excessive stress on one exclusive identity at the expense of others can blot out the complexity involved in national identity formation and lead to diverse kinds of conflict and violence. His conclusion is that Bangladesh, a country where people are predominantly Muslims and speak Bengali, will have to come to terms with the reality that though they can take pride in their language and culture, yet there are minorities living in it whose languages and religions have to be considered and to create conditions whereby they too may flourish if Bangladesh is to remain a cohesive nation. He ends the paper by quoting Sen who noted that "the neglect of the plurality of our affiliations" will inevitably push the country in "the direction of terrifying prospects . . .".

Laiamon Naomi Nengnong, in her paper "Imagery and Reality: Art from the Rohingyas", also seeks to critically look at the Rohingya crisis in Myanmar through the lens of literary expression. In it, Nengnong highlights the questions of identity and belonging, amongst other such questions, that the Rohingyas find themselves in as they face the onslaught of violence and the reality of being reduced to refugees. Rambukwella's perspective of the representation of the refugee in the global discourse of terror as a figure of potential terrror but also desreving empathy is a reminder of the subterranen forms conflict can take. The paper also critically looks at the conceptualization of power from the perspective of a sovereign state and how such views may be used by a state to justify the actions that it takes against its own citizens. This becomes especially pertinent in the case of the Rohingyas as the state effectively becomes the supposed arbiter of life and death, a situation of asymmetrical conflict, similar to the Nepal Civil War cited earlier.

On the other hand, the paper "Gender and Conflict" by Sukalpa Bhattacharjee, seeks to draw our attention to the notion of peace that is oftentimes difficult for women to achieve as they must endure violence that manifests both at a personal as well as at an institutional level. She highlights the plight that women find themselves in as they are often restricted by societies that produce a "hegemonic masculinity" that not only seeks to legitimise gender stereotypes but often also employs violence to restrict female agency. Conflict affects all individuals but the plight of women becomes that much more amplified due to their gender. Lede-e-Miki Pohshna, in "Re-Imagining the Catholic Imagination: Queer, Self and Conflict in Norman E. Pasaribu's *Sergius Seeks Bacchus*" talks about internalised conflict in terms of sexuality within the Catholic Christian framework using Pasaribu's *Sergius Seeks Bacchus*. Pohshna points out that the text is the poet's negotiation with his religious beliefs and his sexuality and in this negotiation he re-imagines God as someone who sanctifies homosexuality, seeing it as the only way of gaining acceptance for his homosexuality. Pohshna points out Pasaribu's subversive interpretation of the sacred via sexuality and links it to the poet's quest of self within his own cultural context. Cr. Patricia Mary Hodge in "Skin Colour Hierarchy: The Ideal Filipina Beauty and the Conflict of Colour", talks about gendered racial discrimination in the Philippines taking into account the legitimization of unrealistic ideal beauty as opposed to realistic forms of beauty. Hodge argues that such skin colour hierarchization in the Philippines is part of the colonial baggage internalised by the population and made the norm which had, in turn, affected the social and economic status of the people, particularly the women. Hodge further points out the role that the global cosmetic market plays in legitimization of skin colour hierarchy that in turn continues to sustain colonial hierarchy of white superiority. While the common reason for conflict in all these three articles is gender, these three authors have also managed to look beyond the situations of conflict and instead try to examine the attitudes/prejudices, beliefs systems that are responsible for such contradictions and perhaps even suggest a change in such attitudes for future social transformations.

Bennathatniel H. Lyngdoh *et al.* and Kaveri Kound look at potential and actual conflicts that are a result of ecological imbalance. Ecological conflict/Environmental conflict is a pertinent area of research within the context of globalisation because of the fragile coexistence that humans share with their present environment. But while conflict can be a result of environmental factors, in their study of the relationship between environmental change, migration and conflict in South-East Asia,

Diengdoh *et al.* find little correlation between conflict and migration that has been caused by environmental disasters or threats. More pressing issues that cause conflict in South-East Asia are ethnic and religious reasons because of the importance of culture for Asians. Diengdoh *et al.* point out that environmental threat is only one factor of migration and that other reasons like economic, political, cultural and social factors play a bigger role in migration and that have potentialities to cause conflict. On the other hand, in the paper "Impact of Ethnic Conflict on Agriculture and Sustainable Rural Development in Bodoland Territorial Area District (BTAD) in Assam", Kaveri Khound highlights how ethnic conflicts, apart from leading to the loss of life and livelihood, leave a lasting impact on the population of an area which leads to increased poverty. This is so because such conflicts, Khound points out, have reduced agricultural production, destroyed agricultural assets and taken away the financial stability of communities. Such conflicts arise out of historical as well as socio-cultural reasons pitting communities against one another. Ethnic conflicts grounded on perceived grievances over identity and belonging ultimately lead to a stake in the claim for the land and its resources. Khound interestingly looks at the effects of conflict on the local ecological balance that in turn affect humans.

An important section of this book is dedicated to a study of conflict in the North-east region of India. Kethoser Kevichusa's paper, "The Naga Story of Conflict", retraces the history of the Naga conflict described by scholars as "the world's longest nationalist conflicts that has claimed thousands of lives", highlighting its historical, geographical and political contours. While some perceived the beginnings of the Naga conflict to be the early twentieth century, yet many Nagas, nationalists and others, claimed that the roots of the conflict can be traced as far back as the earlier half of the nineteenth century, notably the Treaty of Yandabo of 1826. Insightfully written, this paper tries to examine both claims using John Paul Lederach's analysis of 'deeply divided societies' as a lens for looking into and trying to understand the Naga conflict. In the paper "The Khasi Indigenous Beliefs and Christianity: An Encounter or a Negotiation?", Ruth Ibameri Kharbamon seeks to highlight the conflict that arises at a socio-cultural level when indigenous beliefs clash with Westernized Christianity. In her paper, she seeks to trace the influence of Christianity on the Khasi tribe and how that had led to a more globalized outlook. This in turn has led to conflicts with the indigenous faith system that may view Christianity as a force that threatens the indigenous rites and rituals. She highlights how the cultural and spiritual expressions of the Khasis as found in their indigenous belief system are often looked at as expressions of religious symbolism which cannot go hand-in-hand with the practitioners of Christianity in the state of Meghalaya. Her paper seeks to highlight this apparent dichotomy that exists and attempts to see how these conflicts are being navigated within Khasi society. In "Rumours, Suspicions, and the Making of the Narrative: Remembering the Secret Killings in Assam" touches upon a very important event of conflict in Assam during the 1990s, that are a result of ULFA terror attacks. Deka's methodology of research underlines the challenges of field research in situations of violence and trauma that has affected society. True to her argument, Deka shows the usefulness of rumours and suspicions in reconstructing the past, especially when the past is too painful to be articulated with objectivity. The role of memory in reconstructing narratives of conflict and trauma cannot be discounted, despite their selective and arbitrary nature because of the personal experience of the events of conflict and trauma. Deka's paper hints towards another important aspect of studying conflict, namely, its psychological and emotional effects on those involved.

Conflict studies in North-east India shows a lot of potential, because, despite its small geographical expanse in comparison to the subcontinent, it is a region that is multifaceted in its peoples, culture, language, religions as well as colonial and post-colonial experiences. A lot of the situations of conflict in this region can be read under the larger framework of the post-colony and the nation state, yet each situation is different in their contexts. As such, research into situations of conflict in this region is embedded in interdisciplinarity. Further it cannot be denied that conflict studies on North-east India can make important contributions to policy talks on the Act East Policy of the Indian Government. Such an interaction would facilitate in bridging the gap between theory and praxis, bringing together academicians and policy makers with the view of using the insights that will be generated through these deliberations to bring about policies that will benefit the region as a whole.

REFERENCES

Encyclopædia Britannica, inc. (n.d.). *8 deadliest wars of the 21st Century*. Encyclopædia Britannica. Retrieved June 15, 2022, from https://www.britannica.com/list/8-deadliest-wars-of-the-21st-century

Fukuyama, F. (1992). *The End of History and the Last Man*. The Free Press, a Division of Macmillan, Inc.

Galtung, J. (1969). Violence, Peace, and Peace Research. *Journal of Peace Research*, *6*(3196), 167-191. https://doi.org/http://www.jstor.org/stable/422690

Galtung, J. (1970, January 1). *Violence, War, and their Impact. on Visible and Invisible Effects of Violence*. polylog/themes/focus/Johan Galtung: Violence, War, and Their Impact. On Visible and Invisible Effects of Violence. Retrieved June 15, 2022, from https://them.polylog.org/5/fgj-en.htm#s4

Stalenoi, I. (2014, June). *The People's War and Johan Galtung's Conflict Models—UVVG*. Revad. Retrieved June 14, 2022, from https://revad.uvvg.ro/files/nr12/3.Ionut_Stalenoi.pdf

Section I

1
Terror, Affect and Literary Representation

Reflections on Sri Lankan Writing in a South Asian Frame

Harshana Rambukwella

Introduction – the subjective experience of terror

In 1983 when the anti-Tamil pogrom shook the fabric of Sri Lankan civil life, I was just 9 years old – a period from my childhood of which I can generally recall very little. However, I do remember very clearly the date of July 24 when I witnessed plumes of brownish black smoke rise beyond a small range of hills, which separated the suburb where my house was located from the city of Kandy. I asked my father what it was but he seemed equally puzzled as me or feigned puzzlement, knowing what was happening but reluctant to reveal it to me. Later that day in the evening our Tamil neighbours sought refuge with us as a Sinhala mob set their house alight. I am unable to recall with any detail what my feelings were at the time but I think it was more boyish excitement at this unusual and exciting turn of events in what was otherwise a dull suburban middle-class existence. This was one of my very first encounters with terror – a terror deeply implicated in the formation of the post--colonial Sri Lankan nation state and the numerous struggles within it for cultural, political and economic space and recognition.

My second encounter with terror was several years later in the 1987-89 period when southern Sri Lanka witnessed a second Maoist style youth insurrection led by the Marxist Janatha Vimukthi Peramuna (JVP). Twenty-six years ago, before I was born, in 1971, the same group made a failed bid to capture state power and were brutally suppressed by the left-of center government in power at the time. In its second iteration the JVP insurrection was an insidious and violent movement which effectively emasculated the state by spreading a reign of terror throughout the body-politic by carrying out targeted assassinations and killings of those who failed to observe the diktats of the JVP's shadow state – a ghostly administrative machine that imposed nightly curfews, island-wide work stoppages, boycotts of state institutions and functions through the fear of reprisals and corporeal punishment. The state's delayed response in 1989 was equally brutal and insidious. It established death squads that acted with impunity and abducted youth suspected to be JVP members (often targeting political activists of opposition parties) and bodies literally began to litter the streets. A common sight in the morning, as we set off for school, were piles of bodies, shot dead in execution style – either the work of the JVP or the death squads unleashed by the state. Many of the perpetrators of this terror were never persecuted and for many of the families of the victims there has been no closure – bodies never found, killers never identified or punished (Perera, 1995).

A third experience of terror was more distant, but an ever-present danger throughout most of my youth – the haunting figure of the suicide bomber. As the progrom of 1983 led to a full-blown civil war between sections of the Tamil minority community and the largely Sinhala dominated state, the Liberation Tigers of Tamil Elam (or the LTTE) emerged as the single most powerful group within the militant Tamil struggle for statehood. Most of the 1990s and the first decade of the 2000s was dominated by statistics of war dead, numbers dead in suicide blasts and a litany of heads of state and other prominent figures assassinated by the LTTE, including Indian Premier Rajiv Gandhi. The conclusion of this particular articulation of terror in 2009 was something I watched from afar as I was domiciled outside Sri Lanka at the time.

Terror, the nation state and the post-colony

My own life history as a Sri Lankan growing up in post-colonial Sri Lanka therefore has been one deeply implicated and shaped by the presence and effects of terror. As a middle class, urban Sinhala male I was shielded to some extent from the worst effects of terror but what this brief history of terror in Sri Lanka suggests is that terror is something of a foundational category, closely tied to the formation of the post-colonial nation state and therefore of post-colonial subjectivity. I would argue that this is the case for most of South Asia. Emerging from colonialism, the birth of the modern Indian nation state was marked by the bloodletting of the partition and then several decades later came the conflict between West and East Pakistan resulting in the creation of Bangladesh. Also just like the modern history of Sri Lanka post-colonial Indian history is also littered with acts of terror both by the state and non-state actors. In many of these cases, the state's terror is seen and presented as a counter to terror from non-state sources. But as we shall see this narrative masks a history of institutional violence perpetrated by the state that in turn begets terror or terrorism – cause and effect are not so easy to disentangle.

This is apparent in how not all kinds of violence are marked as terror – wars for instance given their statist nature have a certain sanction and legitimacy and are rarely labeled as terror. In the current global discourse on the so-called war on terror, First-World nations attempt to sanction their violence as a just and ethically legitimate response to the threat of 'terror'. Rarely would you come across the term terror associated with the truly horrific campaigns launched by First World nations to 'tame' or 'quell' such terror – such as the ongoing war on terror in parts of the Middle East. At the global level, the narrative of terror maps on to an old Orientalist binary between an enlightened West embattled by an uncivil and barbaric non-West that threatens the West's very existential being. At the same time, this narrative affirms the West's self-identity as civil, progressive and enlightened – anticipated by Edward Said's incisive observation as to how Orientalism though ostensibly about the Eastern Other in reality is about the West's self-perception (Said, 1978). At the national level as Said has also shown us in relation to the Palestinian conflict, the grotesque specter of the Palestinian suicide bomber completely obscures the clinical and structural violence perpetrated by the Israeli regime on Palestinian society condemning it to impoverishment and economic and social stagnation (Said, 2002).

Therefore, in the narrative of nation states, terror is marked as an illegitimate form of violence – a violence that seeks to disrupt the legitimate interests of the nation state and harm its body politic. However, obviously for those individuals and groups that mobilize terror, it is a legitimate means of making themselves heard and a strategy to negotiate with the state – in essence from their perspective it is rationalized as a legitimate use of violence by an oppressed or marginalized group. As is often said "One person's terrorist is the next person's freedom fighter" (Walter, 1969, p. 5). The idea of terror also possibly has some very specific resonances in a place like Assam during the active days of ULFA. Here too, the situation replicates the global discourse of the First World looking at the Third World as a site of terror – while the rest of India looks at the region as one which is characterized by civil unrest and terror, the Assamese experience a double victimization, both by actual terror and the characterization of the region as one of terror and turmoil.

Hence, the normative and received understandings of terror need to be disrupted so as to provoke some thought on how terror operates as a representational category. In doing so, I will specifically draw on how continuities exist between discourses of terror in the colony and what Achille Mbembe (1992) calls the 'post-colony' – essentially the idea that certain forms of power, institutional and representational practices extend from the colonial to the post-colonial and the premise that we cannot understand what some scholars have called the 'post-colonial predicament' (van der Veer and Breckenridge, 1993) without tracing the haunting presence of colonial forms in our contemporary context. As the editors of *Terror and the Post-colonial* observe, "The colonial forms of present-day terror or the *terror of the post-colonial*, we editors submit, demands a turn (back) to certain modes of imperial history in order to understand and to explicate these apparent continuities. In particular 'post-colonial terror' requires that we turn back to the colonial archive of violence and repression, to records of the colonial formations of sovereignty, policing, and surveillance, which find such prominent afterlives in counter-terroristic formations today" (Boehmer and Morton, 2010, p. 7). I will also deploy and extend the notion of grievability as defined by Judith Butler in *Frames of War* where she speaks of how in war situations only some lives and, by default, some deaths become grievable (Butler, 2009). Butler's notion of how media frames war to make some lives more legitimately and affectively grievable than others has direct relevance to terror and its representation as well.

Sri Lankan writing and terror

I will now turn to look at terror specifically in relation to Sri Lankan writing. I am unfortunately only qualified to speak about Sri Lankan writing in Sinhala and English. There is a rich body of Tamil literature dealing with conflict, of which only a very limited amount of material has been translated into Sinhala or English but this corpus of writing will not feature here. There are two major strands in the representation of terror in Sri Lankan writing. One, and the more dominant strand, deals with the ethno-nationalist conflict and is largely written in English. The other is writing which focuses on the Sinhala youth uprisings of the 1970s and 1980s, which I will refer to in passing but not discuss in detail. Sinhala creative writing on the ethnic conflict has been limited – where a kind of normative structural violence that normalizes the conflict exist as in much Anglophone fiction from the late 19th and early 20th centuries where colonialism is taken for granted and rarely discussed explicitly. In Sinhala writing in the rare moments when the ethno-nationalist conflict emerges, it is often seen from an explicitly statist perspective where Tamil militancy is associated with terror and terrorism while the state's violence is seen as a legitimate counter response to this threat of terror. What is often highlighted in this literature is the plight of innocent Sinhala victims, Buddhist monks or village peasantry, who were victims of the terror of the Liberation Tigers of Tamil Elam (LTTE). While undoubtedly the LTTE committed acts of barbaric violence which any ethically conscious society will condemn, the structural conditions that enabled the LTTE's violence rarely figure in these narratives.

This representational bias in Sinhala literature at large derives from the historical formation of the post-colonial Sri Lankan nation state. The dominant political narrative that emerged in Sri Lanka with independence in 1948 was that of seeing the Sinhalese as colonial victims while the Tamils were cast as a privileged minority that had benefitted from colonial governance. Concomitant to this was the romantic notion of a glorious Sinhala pre-colonial past and the task of the post-colonial state was to retrieve and restore the rightful place of the Sinhalese within the nation state (Rogers, 1990; Spencer, 1990). For many Sinhala writers and artists, therefore, the urgent post-colonial task at hand was the promotion of Sinhala culture and identity – evident in the upsurge of Sinhala cultural production in the 1950s in the work of artists such as Ediriweera Sarachchandra, Martin Wickremasinghe and Gunadasa Amarasekara. While none of this work was overtly nationalist in the sense of actively excluding or denigrating Tamil identity or culture, it was blind to how the structures of inclusion and exclusion established in the colony extended into the post-colony. For instance, one of the first major policy acts of the post-colonial nation state was the Citizenship Act of 1948 which effectively made a large population of Indian-origin estate workers who had lived for generations in Sri Lanka effectively stateless. These were colonial victims who were brought to Sri Lanka as indentured labour, doubly victimized in the post-colony. Despite the fact that many Sinhala writers in the 1950s had Leftist leanings there is almost complete silence about this issue in Sinhala writing in the 1950s. However, by the 1970s, partly due to the 1971 JVP uprising, Sinhala cultural production becomes less statist and more critical of the nation state and its structures of inclusion and exclusion. In the Sinhala cinema of the late 1970s leading into the 1980s and 1990s, there is more explicit concern with marginalized figures and communities as the structural violence of the nation state becomes more apparent and is visited upon Sinhala society itself.

Turning to Sri Lankan creative writing in English one can argue that it has always been positioned at a tangent to majoritarian Sinhala nationalism. This is partly due to the fact that English writers came from differing ethno-religious backgrounds and were, therefore, to various degrees, marginalized or victimized by the structural violence of the post-colony. *Emergency 1958* (Vittachi, 1958) was an early expression of the representation of statist violence in English writing. Written in the aftermath of the disastrous consequences of the 1956 Official Language Act which made Sinhala the sole official language of the country despite years of pre-independence debate and discussion on giving Sinhala and Tamil parity status. *Emergency 1958* chronicles the events of 1958 when the country's first post-independence ethno-nationalist violence erupted when Tamil protests about linguistic discrimination were met with politically driven mob violence.

From this point onwards Sri Lankan writers in English regularly produced work which affectively identifies with the plight of ethnic and religious minorities in Sri Lanka. Immediately after the 1983 pogrom, for instance, there is a significant literary production which revisits and reassess the violence of the pogrom but also, at a deeper level, the embedded violence of the nation state itself. The work of Jean Arasanayagam particularly stands out in this context. As a direct victim of ethno-nationalist violence and someone minoritized because of her

Tamil and Burgher identity, her writing from the late 1980s sensitively explores themes of belonging, unbelonging and the structural violence of the nation state (Ho and Rambukwella, 2005). While terror figures as a dominant theme in her writing, it is not the terror of the terrorist or suicide bomber that we are familiar today but the terror of a marginal figure who insistently calls attention upon the precarity of her life. As Judith Butler (2009) reminds us, all of our lives are precarious and can be expunged at will or by accident. But while all humans are positioned precariously, others experience 'precarity' or a heightened level of vulnerability due to their ethnic, class or sexual position in society. While one can, of course, argue that a writer like Arasanayagam did not experience 'precarity' due to her class position that shielded her from the worst of the ethno-nationalist violence, yet revisiting her work offers us a way of rethinking and interrogating the current discourse on terror which silences and suppresses the deep statist and colonial legacies of terror as a category.

The chronicling of violent periods of Sri Lankan history in diasporic Sri Lankan writing is an important phase in Sri Lankan Literature in English. One of the earliest pieces of writing in this category to receive international critical acclaim was *Reef* (1994) by Romesh Gunasekera. Narrated by Triton, a young boy employed as a domestic by a charismatic and bohemian upper middle-class figure, the novel unfolds against a backdrop of increasing political violence in 1970s Sri Lanka. The text has been critiqued for its Orientalist depiction of Sri Lankan society (Perera, 1995) and I would extend this critique to suggest that it participates in a larger narrative of looking at Third World spaces as endemically violent. The title of the novel literally refers to a coral reef – a delicate ecosystem that protects and nurtures a myriad of tropical sea species. By the end of the story both the physical reef and its metaphoric societal counterpart have begun to disintegrate amidst political violence – particularly the violent JVP uprising of 1971. The novel has a prologue where Triton meets a fellow Sri Lankan refugee – someone displaced from Sri Lanka due to later political violence ensuing from the ethno-nationalist conflict in the country and this in turn leads Triton to a reflection on his youth and the events that eventually lead to his life in England. What effectively happens in the narrative is that the two distinct strands of terror as mentioned earlier – terror emanating from ethno-nationalist conflict and terror emanating from Sinhala youth unrest – become conflated and Sri

Lanka becomes a place marked by indistinct and ever-present terror and violence. This representation, feeds into the Orientalist categories of looking at the Third World as a space of uncivility and at the same time obscures the workings of state power and violence. In *Reef,* the violence that is visited upon Triton's master emerges from the frustrations of marginalized Sinhala rural youth – oppressed by both caste and class and the refugee Triton meets in England, is potentially a victim of the Sinhala nationalist state's failure to accommodate the aspirations of the Tamil minority. However, refracted through the limited lens of Triton's first-person narrative all we receive is a sense of an unnamed and unnamable terror residing within a seemingly exotic and benign space. Part of the narrative's critical acclaim internationally, I would argue, is because it affirms this particular view of the Third World.

Two other narratives that address similar themes are Shyam Slevadurai's *Funny Boy* (1994), the coming-of-age story of a young gay boy who while discovering his sexual identity also becomes aware of larger ethno-nationalist tensions in the country and Michael Ondaatje's *Anil's Ghost* (2000) about a Sri Lankan born but Western educated forensic anthropologist who returns to the country to become embroiled in a failed search for restorative justice for a victim of extra-judicial violence. In *Funny Boy,* there is relatively more historical depth compared to *Reef* in terms of how terror figures in the narrative. The terror of ethno-nationalist violence looms as a menacing presence throughout the story and comes to the fore when the novel culminates in the pogrom of 1983. The complicity of the state in ethnic violence is distinctly marked in the story when the lover of the young narrator of the story Arjie's mother, disappears and the police stonewall the investigation. The structural violence of the state is also apparent when a smart young Tamil boy from the North, the son of a friend of Arjie's father, comes to Colombo in search of employment but is eventually hounded out of his position in the leisure industry due to his past associations with the LTTE – an association he has repudiated but is unable to shake off because he is marked as a terrorist in state and societal discourse. However, despite these nuanced accounts of ethno-nationalist violence as Suvendrini Perera (1999) shows the narrative's historical vision is limited – depicting the Sinhala-Tamil conflict as the result of hoary enmity, rather than the product of recent political processes in Sri Lanka's transition from colony to post-colony which has been briefly outlined earlier.

Ondaatje's *Anil's Ghost* deals with the culture of impunity in the 1987-89 period and the thousands of extra-judicial killings that occurred in that period. It is more explicitly critical of both Western representations of Third World spaces and also of statist discourses of terror than *Reef* or *Funny Boy*. As a text *Anil's Ghost* is critically reflective of both the poetics and politics of violence and representation. At one level Anil enters Sri Lanka as a Western trained scientist confident that her training and rational approach to research will enable her to unravel the mysterious death of the skeletal remains of a corpse she is tasked with investigating. However, in collaborating with a local village artist to reconstruct the skeleton's face she discovers that scientific truth and her belief in the possibility of discovering an objective account of history are flawed – forcing her to question her faith in Western epistemology and its methodological approaches. The novel in many ways also forces the reader to confront the banality of international human rights discourse because its investment in a particular place and its local contextual complexities is transient – constantly moving its gaze from one international hot spot to another.

I would like to conclude this section by briefly talking about one more novel, Amabalavaner Sivanandan's *When Memory Dies* (1997) which explicitly resists the expatriate Sri Lankan novel's usual tendency to objectify place and history. Sivanandan's book is epic in its structure and a national allegory of sorts. Unfolding in three large sub-sections it tracks the lives of a group of Sinhala, Tamil and Muslim men and women united by family ties and a commitment to a Left-oriented inclusive Sri Lankan identity. Beginning in the late colonial period it explores through the minutiae of everyday life how colonial modernity and the political processes it unleashes shapes ethno-nationalist politics in the country and from a Leftist vantage trenchantly critiques elite complicity in this process. Explicitly taking what one critic (Perera, 1997) has called a subaltern vantage, it looks at the micro-scale how the state intervenes in the everyday and the consequences of statist violence on Tamil and Muslim minorities. The strength of the book lies in its ability to focalize the precarity of post-colonial existence without sliding into the familiar narrative of Third World uncivility but at the same time construct an ethical position from which to critique the excesses of post-colonial nationalism.

Conclusion – representing terror in a global era of terror

Today in the post 9/11 context of the war on global terror, for many societies terror or specifically the spectre of so-called Islamic terror has become the structural other against which their collective self-identity is increasingly defined. There is a strange and disquieting continuum between the refugee, a forlorn figure of condescension and pity and the terrorist who invokes hatred and revulsion. Both often figure in the Western media as differentially positioned threats to civility, democracy and stability of First World societies. The refugee, a figure for whom the liberal imagination is impelled to feel empathy, is nevertheless also a spectre of terror, though this is rarely articulated as such. As the rhetoric of wall building in the USA suggests refugees specifically and migrants, in general, invoke a sense of disquiet – that one day they might overwhelm their host society. On the other end of the continuum, the refugee or immigrant – both ones that have been denied as well as given entry, emerge as terrorists. If we pause to think, however, both figures are causes of historical entanglements of colonial and imperial exploitation between First and Third World societies. Whether in Pakistan, Afghanistan, parts of Africa or the Middle East, legacies of British and American imperialism feed both the refugee crisis and the veritable explosion in global terror and its effects in European societies.

To conclude, I would like to shift the focus back to South Asia and Sri Lanka. What I tried to track in this piece was how we can critically think of terror as a representational category in South Asian literature. My overarching argument here is that terror cannot be and should not be taken as an ahistorical or decontextualized category. Its presence and visibility in the postcolony owe much to colonial history. One of the tasks we have as critics is to persistently uncover this history when we talk about terror. In doing so we have to be conscious of the global discourse on terror and how it positions us as Third World Asian societies and actively resist the possibility of our writing feeding into the global discourse on terror. However, while doing so we also have an ethical compulsion to resist the normalization of statist terror or the glorification of revolutionary terror. Our history and an awareness of how our post-colonial present is shaped by the predicament of our colonial legacies is critical and important in this task. In Sri Lanka today, there is an urgent task of national reconciliation as a country that has been embroiled in a thirty year long civil war. However, the state of the post--war reconciliation discourse in the country is troubling. Within southern Sinhala society, the spectre of the LTTE suicide bomber has been replaced by that of the emergent Muslim Jihadist – shifting from the demonization of one minority to another, with very little critical consciousness of how minority struggles for self-determination within the nation state are tied to a long history of inequitable post-colonial nation state building. At the same time in relation to the human rights abuses during the last stages of the war concluded in 2009, Sinhala society is readily willing to speak of the terror of Tamil militancy but stridently refuses to acknowledge that the state was complicit in such acts of terror as well. As literary critics we can possibly only play a limited role in such a charged discourse but we need to position ourselves liminally – or what Said called a position between filiation and affiliation. A position where we are nationalist in the sense of being critically alert as to how our societies are depicted and positioned in global or regional discourses but at the same time anti-nationalist in resisting the hegemony of the nation and the state in how it continues to oppress, marginalize and visit terror upon its citizens on the periphery of the nation.

REFERENCES

Boehmer Elleke and Stephen Morton (eds). (2010). *Terror and the Post-colonial.* Blackwell Publishing.

Boehmer Elleke and Stephen Morton. (2010). Introduction to Terror and the Posctolonial. In *Terror and the Post-colonial.* Blackwell Publishing.

Butler Judith. (2009). *Frames of war: When is life grievable?* Verso.

Gunasekera, Romesh. (1994). *Reef.* Riverhead Books.

Ho, Elaine and Harshana Rambukwella. (2006). A question of belonging: Reading Jean Arasanayagam through nationalist discourse. *Journal of Commonwealth Writing, 41*(2), 61-81.

Mbembe, Achille. (1992). Provisional notes on the post-colony. *Arifa: The Journal of the International African Institute, 62*(1), 3-37.

Ondaatje, Anil. (2000). *Anil's Ghost.* Alfred A. Knopf.

Perera, S.W. (1997). Attempting the Sri Lankan Novel of Resistance and Reconciliation: A. Sivanandan's 'When Memory Dies'. *Sri Lanka Journal of the Humanities, 23*(1),13-27.

Perera, Sasanka. (1995). Living with Torturers and Other Essays of Intervention: Sri Lanka Society, Culture, and Politics in Perspective. *Social Scientists Association.*

Perera, Suvendrini. (1999). Unmaking the present, remaking memory: Sri Lankan stories and a politics of coexistence. *Race and Class.*

Perera, Walter. (1995). Images of Sri Lanka through Expatriate Eyes: Romesh Gunesekera's Reef. *The Journal of Commonwealth Literature, 30*(1), 63-78.

Perera, Walter. (1997). Attempting the Sri Lankan Novel of Resistance and Reconciliation: A Sivanandan's 'When Memory Dies'.. *The Sri Lanka Journal of the Humanities*, *xxiii* (1 & 2), 13-27.

Rogers, John D. (1990). Historical Images in the British Period. In *Sri Lanka: History and the Roots of Conflict*, ed., Jonathan Spencer. Routledge, 87-106.

Said, Edward W. (2002). Punishment by Detail, *Al-Ahram*, August, 8-14, 2002. http://weekly.ahram.org.eg/2002/598/op2.html

Said, Edward. (1983). *The World, the Text, and the Critic*. Harvard University Press.

Said, Edward. (1978). *Orientalism.* Penguin.

Selvadurai, Shyam. (1994). *Funny Boy*. Penguin.

Sivanandan, Ambalavaner. (1997). *When Memory Dies*. Arcadia Books.

Spencer, Jonathan. (1990). Introduction: The Power of the Past. In Jonathan Spencer (ed) *Sri Lanka: History and the roots of conflict*, Routledge, 1-18.

van der Veer, Perter and Carol Breckenridge. (1993). *Orientalism and the Post-colonial Predicament.* University of Pennsylvania Press.

Vittachi, Tarzie. (1958). *Emergency '58: The Story of Ceylon Race Riots.* Andre Deutsch.

Walter, Eugene Victor. (1969). *Terror and Resistance: A Study of Political Violence*. Oxford University Press.

2
Confronting Violence Relating to National Identity Formation

A Bangladeshi Perspective

Fakrul Alam

Introduction

It was while studying Shakespeare's *The Merchant of Venice* in school that I first came into contact with the theme of identity and violence in literature, embodied in the character of Shylock. I did not know until then that the New Testament lines, "Eye for eye and tooth for tooth", taken in context, represented Jesus Christ's advocacy of turning the other cheek rather than initiating conflicts that would lead to bloodshed, or at least the attempt to shed blood. I had no clue at that time as well whether Gandhi had said or did not say that the policy of 'An eye for an eye' would leave the whole world blind. What I knew, however, was that when I was taught the text it became clear that Shylock was wrong to insist on his "pound of flesh, no more nor less" (Act IV, Scene 1, 321-322). His scheme to destroy Antonio seemed to me, even at that age, to be completely wrong, completely heinous. But why was it that the scheming, blood-thirsty Shylock attracted the sympathy of all in the class by the time the play ended? It seemed to us schoolboys then that he was a man who had been mistreated by the dominant Christians at least partly because he was an orthodox Jew; even the righteous Antonio had treated him harshly until he needed to borrow money from him, while almost all the Venetian Christians were unsympathetic to him, bordering almost on hatred. And as Muslim boys deeply conscious of an Islamic heritage where dark-skinned North African Muslims had played key parts, it seemed to us too that the treatment of the Prince of Morocco, one of Portia's suitors, was quite prejudiced.

Indeed, the overwhelming impression we got was how wrong it was to have a world like Venice where men who were prosperous and living in a city-state bustling with activity, were suspicious of, and prejudiced against each other either because of race or religion or ethnicity or nationalism. As Shakespeare indicates in his play, Venice was a bustling city then, where people from all over the world converged for trade and commerce, enriching the city-state with a flourishing culture resulting from the mixing and meshing of races and religions. The play left one with a plethora of questions and a deep sense of uneasiness: Why was there so much prejudice and bias? Why were Christians pitted against Jews and wary of dark-skinned Africans? And why did the Jew want his pound of flesh so obsessively? The only thing that seemed right when the play was over was that Lorenzo and Jessica had come together in the last scene of the play to the tunes of music, Shakespeare suggesting thus to us that only love can triumph over hatred created by race or religion!

Reading *The Merchant of Venice* in 1967 Dhaka, at that time the eastern province of Pakistan, sensitized one to the complexities of issues surrounding questions of identity and race and the potential for violence when people start asserting their identities aggressively. East Pakistan, although only a 20 years old province in 1967, had experienced firsthand a number of riots, violent outbursts and bloody attempts to quell dissent over two decades, fueled by the politics of religion, race and language. Disturbing tales of the periodic violent outbursts stemming from political situations associated with national identity formation in the first half of the century, told by elders or read about, left a deep impression on the imagination. It is easy to see from the present-day perspective that in the part of Bengal that had become East Pakistan, identity politics and the conflicts ensuing over them had been quite endemic. What is more, four years later there would be the cataclysm of 1971. Bangladesh would eventually be born in December 16th of that year, after months of bloody conflict ensuing from violence resulting from the Pakistani attempt to prevent Bangladeshis from asserting their rights. Even after the birth of Bangladesh, problems would crop up every now and then because of identity-based politics that led to violence or had the potential for violent outbursts.

In 1967, people living in that space now known as Bangladesh, were part of a Bengal that had been partitioned twice by that time and that had experienced periodic tensions because of the divisions created between peoples by such partitioning as well as lived through the intense violence of the 1940s. After 1947, the country was plunged into recurring episodes of violence in East Pakistan, when Bengalis of the province protested against the imposition of Urdu as the state language in 1952 and when Hindu-Muslim tensions led to violence in 1964. In 1971, the violence was further escalated when the people decided that they did not want to be part of a Pakistan which was going to treat them as second-class citizens and marginalized them politically and economically although they constituted the majority in Pakistan and were bringing in more foreign exchange through their exports. This situation would lead to the third occasion in less than seventy years that this eastern part of Bengal would be partitioned again – on this occasion metaphorically. The third time conflicts would erupt there once again because of identity-based politics, but this time on a scale unprecedented in East Bengal. At the end of 1971, however, Bangladesh finally emerged as an independent and unified country based on one common thread of identity which would ensure any avoidance of major violent conflicts based on identity politics for the overwhelming number of its peoples for at least the immediate future. Minor problems, however, continue to persist and citizens of the country have yet to fully learn about the pitfalls of identity politics in order to avoid and prevent violence against any group of its people based on language, race, or religion. There are things that have been learnt about confronting violence but the challenge will be to learn even more ways of avoiding such conflicts in the future.

The issue of how identity politics has led to violence in Bangladesh is elaborated upon in the following three sections of this chapter. The first of these relate to "Bongobhongo" or the partition of Bengal in 1905, and the tensions created thereby through identity-based politics. Although the partition was annulled in 1911, the division created by it persisted and created tensions and fissures that played a part in the role played by the Muslim politicians in this part of Bengal to opt for the partitioning of the Indian subcontinent in 1947 so that their part of the province could become East Pakistan; The second part focuses on the conflicts beginning with the language issue in 1952 leading to the birth of Bangladesh in 1971; the third reveals the pitfalls that the almost fifty years old nation is beginning to negotiate in the last few decades and the potential for further violence related to identity issues that may reappear in the nation so that the violent outbursts of the past may be avoided in the future, especially in the age of new media, where conflicts can be initiated more easily than before and can go viral in no time at all.

In his work *Identity and Violence: The Illusion of Destiny*, Nobel Laureate Amartya Sen argues how excessive emphasis on a single identity or attempts to scant others can affect national identity formation negatively more often than not since it ignores the fact that identities are inevitably hybrid and always in the process of becoming. Sen argues persuasively that overemphasis on one particular race or class or religious identity can result in not merely divisive but also violent and/or disastrous situations for citizens of nations – especially their minorities – and/or cause endless tension and problems between peoples as well as lead to disruption in lives and give rise to conflicts. Sen has no doubt that a person's identity stems from civilizational cross-currents and is wary of any development that tags a single label on an individual. Any kind of simplistic or definitive categorization of a people, he notes, results from a gross simplification of the nature of human coexistence, and can lead to all sorts of complications and violence in our lives regionally, nationally – and even internationally.

Another thinker/academic whose work has helped in framing this chapter is the Dutch scholar, William van Schendel's essay, "Who Speaks for the Nation? Nationalist Rhetoric and the Challenge of Cultural Pluralism in Bangladesh". The essay provides significant insight into understanding the central conflicts relating to national identity formation in Bangladesh. Schendel's argument here and elsewhere in his writings on Bangladesh is that Bangladeshi political and cultural history is fraught by a central conflict of two ideologies. One of them privileges "ethnicity, religion and sovereignty" and emphasizes the religious roots of the nation that was first affirmed in 1905 (van Schendel, 2001:108). The other stresses "equity, democracy and citizens 'rights'" (ibid) and are rooted in 1952, where protests over the imposition of Urdu as the state language at the expense of Bengali led to massive protests and bloodsheds and an affirmation of the 'Bengaliness' of Bangladeshis as the primary reason for the existence of Bangladesh. The first was behind the decision of leaders in the country who had opted for Pakistan prior to 1947, and leaders who took over in

November 1975 after the assassination of Sheikh Mujibur Rahman and were behind the establishment of successive military or quasi-military governments. The first of these two governments was the one led by General Ziaur Rahman till his assassination on May 30, 1981. The second of them was led by General H.M. Ershad till he was deposed from power through a mass uprising in 1990. Afterward, Bangladesh has been ruled either by the Bangladesh Awami League, the party led by the man widely acknowledged to be the "father of the nation", Sheikh Mujibur Rahman, and the man who was assassinated by rebellious military men on August 15, 1975. It is a party that stresses what van Schendel calls "establishment nationalism" (128), and prioritizes the democratic, socialist, secularist as well as nationalistic ideals of Mujib. The other party that alternated in power with it after winning the first election held after the collapse of the dictatorial Ershad regime in 1991 is the Bangladesh Nationalist Party (BNP). According to Schendel, this party has upheld the "post--communalist strain" of Bangladesh nationalism, stressing religion as the key component of Bangladeshi national identity formation. The violence related to identity politics in Bangladesh may thus, be read through the lens of van Schendel's concept as outlined in his essay.

The First Partition of Bengal and Questions of Identity till Partition (1905-1947)

In any narrative retelling of identity-based politics in Bangladesh in recent history, "Bongobhongo" or the partitioning of Bengal in 1905 has to play an originary part, for in many ways it initiated the traumas, tensions and fissures that kept cropping up subsequently and caused ideological conflicts which would at times, have violent consequences. The partitioning itself, however, was the result of any number of causes though Lord Curzon, Viceroy of India at that time, cited administrative necessity as the primary reason for dividing Bengal into two parts. The Muslim leaders of the eastern parts of Bengal, for their part, mostly welcomed the move since it would give them the kind of prominence that a Kolkata-based power apparatus had denied them. The thought of autonomy inspired them in trying to uphold the partition and support the idea of having their centre of administration in Dhaka. Clearly, they felt that a province of their own would empower them in a way not possible in a West Bengali Hindu dominated, Kolkata-centred Bengal. But once the new province of "Eastern Bengal and Assam" was created on 19 July, 1905, agitation against partition, led by highly educated Hindus, gathered momentum rapidly. Many of them felt that the partition of Bengal was a perverse attempt to stifle a burgeoning nationalist movement centred in Kolkata that had as its goal, empowerment of Indians who were beginning to assert themselves against imperial rule and were uniting against the British to claim self-rule. To them, Lord Curzon was initiating a "divide and rule" policy and undermining the unity of Bengal and the centring of Indian politics as well as Bengali culture in Kolkata. Amongst Hindus, there was a move to assert 'Bengaliness', self-rule, and the image of a motherland in distress gathered momentum, although a very Orthodox Muslim man, family history tells us, had taken part in the *swadeshi* movement, showing that there were exceptions in the divide that proved that Muslims too could opt to be against Bongobhongo. To take one example of how Kolkata-based Hindu or Brahmo Bengalis, even the most liberal of them, enrolled in a campaign that would gather immense momentum by the day, we can cite the case of Rabindranath Tagore, who joined it energetically and imaginatively, composing poems and songs to prop up the movement; he also took part in meetings and processions organized for that purpose.

Tagore eventually withdrew from the *swadeshi* movement, disillusioned by its excesses, its increasing inclination to veer towards violence, and its prioritizing of Hinduism at the expense of the Muslims of rural Bengal, whom he had come to know well while looking after his landed estates in East Bengal. Nevertheless, the movement itself had gathered so much strength that the British were forced to annul the partition of Bengal within five years and reunite the province in 1911. In fact, with the Congress Party asserting the unity of all Indians, regardless of religion, caste, or class, and embracing the ideal of non-violent protests, the movement was transformed into a movement of independence that would gather momentum exponentially in the next four decades.

However, the partition of Bengal in 1905 had created the seed of divisions between the Hindus and Muslims of Bengal and had opened up wounds that would not heal easily. Not a few Bengali Muslims had become embittered about the way they had been disempowered. It was to assuage them that the University of Dhaka (DU), was created by the British to somehow make up to them for having been disempowered so suddenly. In the words of the first Chancellor of Dhaka, Lord Lytton, DU was established by the British as a "splendid imperial compensation" (Chaudhury, 1988: 26) for the Muslims of Bengal. Subsequently, the Muslim League would draw on their disenchantment by emphasizing the way they had been deprived of their rights and were once again being forced to play second fiddle to Kolkata-based politicians, especially Hindu ones. The emphasis on the dangers of having their Islamic identity subsumed by a Hindu-tinged Indian identity in a country destined to be ruled by the people who constituted the overwhelming majority resonated with the majority of the population in East Bengal. In that sense, the short-lived partition of 1905 had given Muslims a sense of empowerment that had consequences that were long lasting.

Indeed, between 1905 and 1937, identity-based politics amongst Hindus and Muslims throughout Bengal became viral even as the "Quit India" movement against the British of the Congress and the mobilization of Muslims clamoring for a separate country, as well as against British rule, gathered momentum. Having to deal with the war situation in Europe as well as the Indian independence movement in India, the British declared their plans to quit India post-haste. Their subsequent policies as well as increasing communal divides resulted in identity-based political violence in both parts of Bengal. In *Identity and Violence: the Illusion of Identity*, Amartya Sen recalls his "disturbing memories of Hindu-Muslim riots in India in the 1940s" and notes how even in the "bewildered eyes of the child" that he was then, he could see "the massive identity shifts that followed divisive politics" (9). Sen notes the ensuing "carnage" (170) in Kolkata because of communal tensions that had erupted on 16 August, 1946 during what is now known as "the 1946 Calcutta Killings" though he failed to mention the Noakhali riots of the period afterward that became so bloody and destructive that Mahatma Gandhi felt that he had to go to that then quite remote district to quell the riots and spread his message of peace.

Sheikh Mujibur Rahman, fondly called both "Bangabandhu" or "Friend of Bengal" and "Father of the Nation" in Bangladesh, was then in Kolkata as a staunch Muslim Leaguer and adherent of H.M. Suhrawardy. His *Unfinished Memoirs*, a work that he had written during a long prison term and left unfinished, depicts him patrolling the Muslim quarters of Kolkata during the communal riots that had erupted there in 1946 to defend the people there. Although staunchly on the side that would demand partition, he is clearly shocked at the fratricidal violence that had ensued. As he puts it in the section on the Kolkata riots of the *Unfinished Memoirs*:

> Calcutta city streets seemed to be strewn with dead bodies. Neighborhood after neighborhood was in flames. It was a horrible scene! That people could treat each other in this way was too frightening a thought. (68, translation mine).

Mujib notes how the Kolkata riots had a chain effect. They led to the one in Noakhali, which in turn led to the riots in Bihar. He soon volunteered to take part in the relief work undertaken there by the Muslim League government. Not a few pages of the *Unfinished Memoirs* deal with the horrors of the Bihar and the Kolkata riots. These pages imply that Mujib had been sobered by them and would now begin to see Hindu-Muslim relationships from a perspective that would make him stress amity as a goal for Muslims as well as Hindus when he came to an East Bengal that would soon become East Pakistan on the eve of partition.

The violence ensuing from identity-based politics in the pre-partition period of East Bengal's history also finds resonance in literature as seen in the poem "1946-47", by Jibanananda Das, the greatest Bengali modernist poet. Das loved riverine east Bengal but the fear of partition-related violent outbreaks among educated East Bengali Hindus drove his family to Kolkata in the 1940s, where he witnessed the riots of 1946 and the tension and suspicion as well as the violence that led to partition. The situation led him to penned these poignant lines and I read them in my translation:

> …all are suspicious of each other.
> Creation's darkest thought seems to be – malice.
> Creation's dearest thought: inducing pain

No doubt thinking about the religious riot dead bodies he had seen in Kolkata streets in 1946, he wrote these moving lines in "1946-47":

> They sleep on.
> If I would call them, billowing forth from the bloody river,
> They would come close to me and say, "I am Yasin,
> Hanif, Muhammed, Makbul, Karim, Aziz –

And who are you?" Putting their hands on my chest,
Raising eyebrows, the river of blood overflowing,
They would say: "Gagan, Bipin, Sasi, of Pathurgata,
Of Maniktala, Sham Bazar, Ghalib Street, of Entaly – "
Who knows from where they had come; people from
The lowest rung of life.... (Das, my translation, 117).

Identity Related Politics and Violence in East Pakistan – 1947-1971

Partition meant that people like Sheikh Mujibur Rahman would opt to be in the part of Bengal that they had championed until it became East Pakistan. But it did not take him and others of his generation long to discover that the divisions and violence created by identity politics centred on religion needed to give way to another kind of identity-based politics, one based on linguistic as well as political and economic considerations. Mujib, in fact, was among the Bengali student activists at a huge public rally in post--partition Dhaka in 1948, when Mohammed Ali Jinnah, "the father" of the nascent nation of Pakistan, declared at a mammoth public rally that "the state language of Pakistan is going to be Urdu and no other language". The reaction to his declaration was one of instant and immense disappointment amongst the audience, particularly the students who had gathered to hear him; it was immediately evident that the Bengalis present there were not ready to accept the imposition of Urdu as the only state language in a part of the country where almost every one spoke Bengali. It was soon evident too that though Pakistan had been created on the basis of Muslim religious identity, and though Muslims in East Bengal had affiliated themselves with the cause of Pakistan till their part of the world had become East Pakistan, they were not going to have their mother tongue become subordinated to Urdu just because they were Muslims.

From this point onwards, the history of Bangladesh took a turn where linguistic nationalism overwhelmed the religious nationalism that had led the Muslim politicians of Bengalis to opt for Pakistan. The students of DU were at the heart of the protest, and Mujib was one of their most visible and inspirational leaders. But Pakistan's administrators ignored the growing resentment against their arbitrary diktats and hardened in their resolve to make Bengalis accept an identity where Urdu would be their linguistic marker and not Bengali.

The next couple of years saw Bengalis in East Pakistan rallying for the rights of their language and the (West) Pakistani leaders insisting on having a state language that they associated with Islam and thought was purer in a way they felt Bengali could not be. Mujib was one of a number of student leaders who were imprisoned by the Pakistani rulers to stifle dissent but things came to a head when Khwaja Nazimuddin, the Prime Minister of Pakistan at that time, reaffirmed officially a few years later on January 27, 1952 that Urdu would be the main state language of the country.

If there is one originary moment in the birth of Bangladesh, it has to be February 21, 1952 when agitating Bengali students who had chosen an All-Party Central Language Action Committee to uphold the cause of Bengali as a state language called for a general strike protesting Khawza Nazimuddin's declaration. They marched en masse towards the legislative assembly building which was in session then. They had decided to protest in a manner that would make the Pakistani government and the members of the assembly withdraw the high-handed decision. But when the alarmed Pakistani administrators decided to stifle the dissenting students decisively by firing point blank at them, five of them died on the spot while hundreds were injured. The outcry that ensued in the whole of East Pakistan against the Pakistani administration made it withdraw the order that had relegated the Bengali language to the margins. However, Bengalis would be inspired by the examples of their language martyrs to assert the Bengali part of their identity in all possible ways from then on. From that day, the 21st of February began to be celebrated annually as Shaheed Dibosh or simply "Ekushey February". It became, in effect, "the day of the martyrs", a day of remembrance, and an annual occasion to pay tributes to the fallen. But it also became a day to reaffirm the Bengali identity of East Pakistan from 1954 onwards and the day to pledge anew to preserve and flourish it. A newly elected East Pakistani provincial government set up the Bangla Academy in 1955; a Shaheed Minar or martyr's monument was also erected in 1966 after a previous one had been demolished, although it too would be destroyed in 1971 by the Pakistani Army, only to be rebuilt in a liberated Bangladesh.

Indeed, one can say with hindsight that the movement to carve out a nation for Bengalis based on their 'Bengaliness' began in earnest from the 21st of February, 1952 and gained momentum by the day from then on till 1971. The Bengalis in Pakistan, far from being deterred by the brutality of the Pakistan response to their demand to make Bengali a state language, redoubled their efforts to establish it and succeeded in making the Pakistanis give in to their demand. They had successfully confronted the violence engineered by the Pakistanis and had shown how brutal force was not only to be resisted but also overcome for a just cause. In fact, Ekushey became a powerful stimulus for a generation of East Bengali intellectuals, writers and artists. It gave rise to stirring poems, songs, fiction and prose. Research on the origins and evolution of Bengali and the history of Bengali folklore and literature in this part of Bengal took off from this point as never before. It was clear that one could affirm one's identity not violently but through cultural activism and engaging with creative outlets such as poetry, creative prose, music and the visual arts.

From the mid-1950s onward, progressive views thus held sway in what was then East Pakistan. Under the leadership of the Awami League, what van Schendel called "establishment nationalism" which prioritizes the democratic, socialist, secularist as well as nationalistic ideals articulated by Mujib, dominated the imagination of the overwhelming number of Bengalis, regardless of their religion, caste or class. The Pakistani government, from 1958 onwards dominated by the military, first under General Ayub Khan, and then when he was deposed by a popular uprising led by Mujib in 1969, General Yahya Khan, ruled Pakistan, attempting to revive what van Schendel called the "post-communalist strain" still dormant in some Bangladeshis, prioritizing Islamic values, and taking every opportunity to play the Islamic card. The government and its East Pakistani lackeys kept declaring that Islam was in danger, and stressing that India was attempting to encroach on East Pakistani territory, and that secularism and cultural activism were not only subversive to Pakistani values but also in subterranean ways propping up pro-Indian Mujib and the establishment nationalists. There were communal riots in 1950 and 1964 in response to communal riots in India, seemingly allowed up to a point by a government working to prop up the communalist strain and discredit Indian politics and identify it with communalism.

Nevertheless, Mujib and the Awami League and left-leaning parties, kept rallying and succeeded in overcoming obstacles massed in their way and in mobilizing the masses for a democratic and secularist nationalist mandate, with the Bengali language and culture being key markers. The military government's attempts to use a carrot and stick policy in response, in addition to playing the Islamic card, did not work. Mujib's "6-points demand", emphasizing a federated Pakistan, a parliamentary system of government based on direct franchise, and emphasizing representative government based on direct voting and autonomy for the provinces and downgrading the role the army could have in provincial affairs, appealed to people. So did the idea of delinking religion to state policy and emphasizing the role of upholding cultural autonomy and the mother tongue. A truly fair election held on 10 December, 1970 confirmed that the overwhelming majority of Bangladeshis believed in the values of "establishment nationalism" and a nation where language, culture and democratic values had priority over authoritarian governments making use of Islam to hold on to power desperately.

The Pakistan Army, where Bengalis were recruited in proportionately small numbers, decided after the elections, with the help of Zulfiqar Ali Bhutto, to deny Mujib and the Awami League the right to rule, though the latter had got an absolute majority in the elections. The Pakistani army, it has to be said, grew out of the myth of the "martial race" and seemed bent on propagating it. The myth, as has been often pointed out by historians writing about the Indian mutiny and its military consequences, spread the idea that the British Indian Army should recruit only from the "martial races" and avoid "non-martial people" in building their army, although if one deconstructed the labels, it was clear that the concept favoured loyalists to the British throne, and not those soldiers belonging to regiments who had led the uprising in 1857, or parts of India where anti-British sentiments were strong. The Pakistani army continued in this vein to recruit from the western wing and so in 1971 was overwhelmingly West Pakistani in its composition and all set to execute the bloody policy of subjugating the supposedly non-martial but subversive East Pakistanis. They were supported in their murderous endeavours throughout 1971 by the Jamat-e-Islami, the East Pakistani branch which was the only major party to collaborate actively with the Pakistani army to uphold Pakistan and communalist nationalism.

In March, 1971, Mujib was captured, the Awami League-led establishment nationalist leaders put into jail, and Islam and communalist values blown out of proportions in justifying army rule and brutality. The canard of "Islam is in danger" was spread throughout East and West Pakistan to justify brutality. But the Pakistani Army's machinations did not work, and with the Indian Army's intervention, the lack of any support from the overwhelming number of Bengalis of East Pakistan, and the Mukti Bahinis' insurgent operations and active support in backing up the Indian army and proactive role in field operations, Bangladesh was liberated. Religion-based identity politics was discredited decisively and the Jamat-e-Islami banned. Secularist, pro-Bangladesh values triumphed over religious communalist ones. To adapt Amartya Sen's observations in his "Prologue" to *Identity and Violence: The Illusion of Destiny*, Bangladeshis had shown in 1971 that the Pakistani attempt at "the imposition of an allegedly unique identity" was "a crucial component of the 'martial art' of fomenting sectarian confrontation" (xiii). The outcome proved that such an attempt did not lead to the desired results of thwarting the Bangladesh independence movement. To adapt Sen's comments in his "Prologue" once again: Bangladeshis were not willing to opt for a country "categorized according to some *singular and overarching* system of partitioning" (Sen, xii).

Identity Related Politics and Intermittent Violence in Bangladesh in the last Four Decades

From December 1971 to August 15, 1975, Bangladesh was a country going ahead with the values associated with "establishment nationalism". As van Schendel had identified and as quoted earlier, these were values centring on "equity, democracy and citizens 'rights'". These were the values that were behind the four pillars of the 1972 constitution of the nascent republic – nationalism, democracy, secularism and socialism. Clearly, Bangladeshis under Mujib's guidance and with the experience of the whole liberation movement behind them had opted for a country where identity was not based on what Sen in his book called "solitarist" principles (ii).

Unfortunately for Bangladeshis, Mujib was brutally assassinated on August 15, 1975, along with most members of his family. Four major leaders of his party were killed in jail on November 3, 1975, by mutineers working according to a plan to weed out establishment nationalism values and reintroduce communalist ones. After a series of coups and counter-coups, General Ziaur Rahman, a liberation war hero, stepped in to what was apparently a power vacuum. The values of the establishment nationalists were put under the rug, so to speak, and the "post-communalist strain" of Bangladesh nationalism that prioritized Islam and scanted the four pillars of the 1972 constitution became the ruling dogma. Zia revoked the ban on the Jamat-e-Islami soon after coming to power and they united with his party in elections.

From this point onwards, the BNP, formed by Zia to contest elections, collaborated with the Jamatis, and did everything possible to spread "communalist" nationalism. BNP was in power as long as Zia was alive (he died in a coup in May 1990), and then when democracy returned to Bangladesh in 1991, from then to 1996 and once again from 2001 to 2006. The BNP and the Jamatis worked in tandem to emphasize the Islamic roots of Bangladesh and downplay the secularist strain in its politics. With its active support and that of international Islamist organizations bent on establishing a globally resurgent Islam, not only the Jamat but also other Islamic agencies, seminaries and organizations sprung up throughout the country, clearly bent on emphasizing as well as prioritizing Islam in the Bangladeshi state.

The BNP and the Jamatis alternated in power with the Awami League and its left-leaning and secularist allies after the 1990s (1996-2001 and 2008). In fact, and as is well known, the Awami League has been in power in Bangladesh after elections were held on 29 December, 2007. In government, it has tried to re-establish and implement the establishment nationalist agenda to the best of its ability, given a global scenario of resurgent Islam and rightist politics, but has also conceded some ground to Islamists in affiliating with some Islamist parties. Nevertheless, the BNP, along with the Jamatis and other extreme right wing Islamist parties, tried to force their way back to power through violent tactics in 2013 and 2014, only to be thwarted by the Awami League government in power, which was able to have the army back it fully and which became somewhat authoritarian in the process. Young and secular-minded nationalists tried to put the Jamatis on the dock, literally so, by protesting a life and not a death sentence handed out to a Jamati leader who in 1971 had been guilty of many murders. This was what was behind the Shahbagh movement of 2013, where demonstrators demanded that he and other "war criminals" be given capital punishment. But in late February, 2014, the Islamist forces counter-attacked and it needed drastic intervention by the government to avoid further internecine conflict between the establishment nationalist and the post-communalist groups.

Other than the violence, the brutal deaths in coups and counter-coups, the assassination of top ranking leaders, and execution of ordinary soldiers and civilians as well as card-carrying party members, Bangladesh has seen deaths and violence from identity based politics in other ways and spheres too. These include attempts by government forces to quell insurgency in the Chittagong hills, where General Zia initiated a policy of settling Bengali Muslims from chars, or newly emerged or low-lying, flood and tidal wave prone land/islands in the sea belt of Bangladesh amongst the hill people. Already marginalized because of the construction of the Kaptai Dam in 1962 and the flooding that resulted then, they would take up arms for a while till a peace treaty was signed. Here again were people who had felt that their identities and lifestyles had been threatened by others, in this case lowlanders helped by a government that had interfered with their lives, marginalized them, disrupted their economy and disturbed their environment.

There has been periodic violence in Bangladesh funded through religious fundamentalists. Communalist feelings have been repeatedly stoked by overseas extreme right and militant Islamist parties in recent decades. The results were that in some cases Islamic fundamentalists have organized themselves into armed groups to adopt guerilla tactics in vulnerable areas, at times forcing the state to combat them brutally. In other cases, they have adopted tactics which are more violent in many ways by attacking and murdering expatriates and foreign visitors in a manner that would grab international attention. The most deadly and notorious of such attacks is one that took place in a posh area of Dhaka in a café known for its fraternizing of foreigners and well-off Bangladeshis. The Holey Artisan Bakery incident of 2017, as it was known, was widely covered by the international media, with 29 people killed overnight, including 18 foreigners and 2 locals, some of the bakery staff and the five gunmen.

Another tactic adopted by fundamentalist Islamists of the extremist and violent persuasion has been to target bloggers who have articulated their radical or free-thinking beliefs on social media. Indeed, the militants have been initiating social-media orchestrated violence every now and then, concocting incidents or blowing minor or de-contextualized comments or events out of proportion to indicate how Islam was being belittled and Muslims threatened or insulted for their religious beliefs by people from minority communities. In one such recent incident, four people were killed and scores of others injured in the island of Bhola, this time the victims being the religious zealots themselves. They had been shot by the police, which had acted in desperation at the outburst of the zealots and their mobilization intending to attack the minority Hindu community over an alleged aspersion to Islam in Facebook. There were similar episodes of identity related violence in the recent past, flamed through social media in Ramu, Coz's Bazar, against Buddhists as well. Such incidents uncover the ever-present threat of militants with communalist affiliations in Bangladeshi politics in its extreme form, attempting to destabilize the state and create mob frenzy against any signs of secularism or perceived threats or insults to the dominant religion.

A pertinent point to be noted is that this chapter on violent conflicts triggered by identity politics in Bangladesh has been confined solely to domestic conflicts. This is because Bangladesh has not been involved in conflicts with other countries in the region. However, in the recent decades, there has been tension because of the influx of Rohingyas, triggered by violence between the Rohingya Muslims and Myanmar Buddhists that have led thousands and thousands of them to flee their native land, opt mainly for Bangladesh as well as other neighbouring South-east Asian countries, thereby, creating tension and an unstable and difficult situation in south-eastern Bangladesh.

Lessons Learnt or Being Learnt in Bangladesh from Identity-Related Conflicts and Violence

As has been felt by many and articulated best by the British novelist Aldous Huxley in introducing his dystopian novel, *Brave New World* to a CBS radio audience in 1956, "The price of liberty, and even of common humanity, is eternal vigilance". Bengalis in the eastern wing of what was once Bengal, then East Pakistan and is now Bangladesh, have learnt the hard way, and are still learning that nothing ensures permanent peace. There is no end to conflict or permanent solutions to fissures created by identity-based politics, whether because of issues related to religion, language, race, or economic/political issues. The call, as Huxley puts it, is for "eternal vigilance". There are no easy solutions, no panacea that will guarantee perpetual amity between peoples. But one must learn from Rabindranath's disillusionment with the extremism of nationalist politics, Gandhi's policy of non-violence and peace disseminated to those affected in riot-torn Noakhali, Mujib's discovery that overemphasizing one part of identity in dealing with other people is to risk one's humanity and promote communal violence. One must learn from the incident of February 21st in Bangladesh never to force one group's language or religious and cultural values on another, and to recognize that we all live in a world where we must live together despite our divergent identities, by working for peace and harmony. In the final analysis, what seems to be evident is that those who enshrined secularism and democracy as well as nationalism and socialism as the pillars of Bangladesh's constitution in 1972, had got it right. It is greatly unfortunate that Bangladesh's erstwhile leaders, whether General Zia or General Ershad, removed secularism and interfered with democratic norms so that the country has never been able to recapture completely the spirit of the 1972 constitution with its secular and democratic overtone. With additional problems fomented by new developments such as social media and its potential for both good and evil, every citizen is responsible to use this two edged sword positively, whether nationally, regionally or internationally, to minimize conflict, promote communal harmony and promote internationalism.

A shining example may be found in Rabindranath Tagore's Viswa-Bharati, an intellectual space, "where the world makes a home in a single nest", and where scholars and creative writers from north and south and east and west could come together to do work that promotes harmony between peoples, learn from history and each other's cultures, and negotiate a path through problems that are bound to creep up sooner or later, by exemplary dedication to peace, non-violence and creative and meaningful work. To make a nest of the whole world and a world without borders! And as Amartya Sen notes: "The neglect of the plurality of our affiliations and of the need for choice and reasoning obscures the world we live in [and] pushes us in the direction of terrifying prospects portrayed by Matthew Arnold in 'Dover Beach':... We can do better than that"! (xiv).

REFERENCES

Chaudhury, Serajul Islam. (1988). *Dhaka University: The Convocation Speeches, Vol. 1, 1923-1946.* University of Dhaka Publications.

Das, Jibanananda. (2003). *Jibanananda Das: Selected Poems.* Second and expanded edition. (Fakrul Alam, Trans.). University Press Ltd.

Rahman, Sheikh Mujibur. (2013). *Unfinished Memoirs.* (Fakrul Alam, Trans.). University Press Ltd.

Sen, Amartya. (2006). *Identity and Violence: The Illusion of Identity.* Allen Lane.

Shakespeare, William. (Ed.1997). *The Merchant of Venice*. In M.M. Mahood (Ed.), Cambridge UP.

van Schendel, Willem. (January 2001). Who Speaks for the Nation? Nationalist Rhetoric and the Challenges of Cultural Pluralism in Bangladesh. *Geopolitics,* 101-147.

3
Imagery and Reality
Art from the Rohingyas

Laiamon Naomi Nengnong

Conflict, whether amongst small communities or larger ones, on the basis of race, religion, or any other factor of discrimination is not new to world history. In fact, regardless of the many claims that human society has progressed over the years, disruptions in the social order occur and re-occur on the basis of the same kind of factors of discrimination that have existed perhaps centuries ago. The Rohingya people are victims of such a kind of discrimination and conflict. Many Rohingya poets have made the act of writing poetry – a medium through which all the issues pertaining to the horrible experiences they have had to endure as a people, is disseminated to the global community that is willing to listen. They speak of exclusion, racism, social identity, displacement, the self in relation to the other. Rohingya poets who have fled the military regime such as Saiful Rohin, express a sense of isolation and unbelonging, in any place that a refugee makes a new home in the lines from his poem, "I was a refugee no one wanted":

> "...In various places, I was asked 'where are you from?'
> My reply was 'it's Burma' with a political storm.
> I was told I belonged nowhere,
> leaving me crying for a safe place anywhere.
>
> It was time no one wanted us in Asia.
> For me, it was so difficult to be in Malaysia.
> The life as a refugee worse than being in jail, a living hell.
> I often asked myself when justice will prevail?..."
>
> (Rohin, *The Art Garden Rohingya*)

In an essay *Unmaking Home*, Claudette Lauzon speaks of the alterations in the meaning given to a home or the idea of a home and homeliness in contemporary art, as well as in the 'world of trauma' that we live in. Lauzon opines that modern and contemporary art presents a home as a "fractured, fragile, or otherwise unsettled space of impossible habitation" owing to the history of displacement that has become a global social phenomenon. Displacement in our age of "unprecedented mobility" and "mass migration" involve "...oppressive and alienating experiences of exile, asylum, immigration, internal displacement, and statelessness." The writer further states, "Home, for the millions of displaced and disenfranchised citizens of the world, is inextricably linked to loss." The Rohingya sense of home can be seen as something fragmentary similar to Homi K. Bhabha's expostulation of "unhomeliness" in *The World and the Home*. Bhabha explains the merging of the shrinking world of "domesticity" of James' Isabel Archer into becoming a site "for history's most intricate invasions" (p. 141). The idea of home is henceforth, that of impermanence and that which must be replaced often; because of extreme social and political disruptions. Emotions and sentimentalities associated with the houses that have been burned, in the Rohingya context, become part of the "psychic history" of the Rohingya, and is the burden that they carry over the borders.

The terms "genocide" and "obliteration" are constantly used in the discussions related to the Rohingya. A neo-Nazism wave seems to be surrounding certain sections of society in Myanmar. In a news article entitled *Hitler/Nazi symbols are popular in Myanmar and now Men Kampf is made accessible in Burmese* (Zarni, 2017) it is reported that Nazi symbols are very openly used with no public objections "by those who want to exterminate Rohingyas in particular and all Muslims in general" (Zarni). Even political leaders and the intelligentsia are reported to have spoken in "genocidal discourses". The mass killings in Myanmar never spared even young children. Tun Khin, a Rohingya human rights activist has called Coz's Bazaar camps a "concentration camp". The imposition of a two-child policy which was passed in the year 2013, was applied only on the Rohingya while Buddhists in Rakhine state were exempted of this. Extreme rightist groups like the 969 have referred to people of the Rohingya community as "dogs" and propagate the belief that Rohingyas are "subhuman". The racial, religious *othering* amongst Burmese people and monks alike; the *us vs. them* perception against the Rohingya minority is so rampant. Thus, the theory of the *Other* or *Otherness* is interweaved with the Rohingya experiences of genocide, racial and ethnic cleansing.

John A. Powell, in his article, *Us vs. Them: The sinister techniques of 'Othering'—and how to avoid them* explains *othering* in these words:

> When societies experience big and rapid change, a frequent response is for people to narrowly define who qualifies as a full member of society – a process I call '*othering*'... *Othering* is not about liking or disliking someone. It is based on the conscious or unconscious assumption that a certain identified group poses a threat to the favoured group. It is largely driven by politicians and the media, as opposed to personal contact. Overwhelmingly, people don't "know" those that they are *Othering*. (Powell, *The Guardian*)

Foucault in his *Society must be defended* lectures, spoke extensively on "state racism", wherein he explains that racism and war take place once the 'biological' is under the control of the state. One's right to life and death (which were attributes of Sovereignty) become 'strange rights' as Foucault concludes that the right to life and death is not in the subject's hand – "in terms of his relationship with the sovereign the subject is by rights neither dead or alive" – but rather in the hands of the sovereign. The power of the sovereign is to either put people to death or let them live; these two factors not being taken as "natural or immediate phenomena" and neither are they those that fall "outside the field of power" (Foucault, p. 240). Foucault explains the right of the power of the sovereign and its effect on life as follows:

> Sovereign power's effect on life is exercised only when the sovereign can kill. The very essence of the right of life and death is actually the right to kill: it is at the moment that the sovereign can kill that he exercises his right over life. It is essentially the right of the sword. So there is no real symmetry in the right over life and death. Nor is it the right to allow people to live or to leave them to die. It is the right to take life or to let live. And this obviously introduces a startling dissymmetry. (Foucault, p. 241)

Racism, as Foucault defines it, is a “break” into the sphere which is under the control of power; a “fragmenting” of the field of the biological which is controlled by power. The distinction, strife and hierarchy amongst races, as well as the categorization of what is superior or inferior, is due to a “biological type caesura” in the domain of the biological. The function of racism is to “fragment, to create caesuras within the biological continuum addressed by biopower” (p. 255). Racism follows the idea that if more deaths are permitted, then the more chance one gives to his own survival. It undeniably stems from what defines a war, in which enemies are killed for one to live. In racism, however, the relationship between the life of oneself and that of the other is not ‘military’ but a relationship of ‘biological type’. This implies that the more the race that is seen as inferior or abnormal becomes exterminated, the more the superior I as individual or race, can live and thrive. The inferior’s death, or the death of the other, does not so much guarantee safety but yet ensures still, the healthier and “purer” life. When there is a normalizing of the act of extermination by a society, even killing on the basis of race becomes legitimized, herein, the state enters a “biopower mode” by which the act of killing becomes a “state function.” Racism is then the “pre-condition for exercising the right to kill”. Foucault further says “if the power of normalization wished to exercise the old sovereign right to kill, it must become racist”. (p. 255, 256). This idea can be used to analyze the Holocaust, and the racism or othering in the context of Myanmar in relation to the Rohingya man as well.

Foucault expounds that in the case of the Nazi state, the “biopower” that is exerted by the state or the right of the sovereign to kill anyone could also mean the right to kill other people and also the state’s own. The state has designed that the field of biological life that it guarantees safety, security, and manages has to succumb to its right over the death of individuals and even the right to be exposed to death. The state then became an “absolutely racist, murderous and suicidal” as the extermination of a racial other costed the German man’s own living conditions (p. 260).

Mayyu Ali, a poet and activist who runs the Youth Empowerment Centre in the refugee camp, in his poem “A Rohingya Refugee” speaks of the kind of *othering* that every refugee suffers, in living and in dying:

> I can be killed here in Bangladesh.
> My body can earn a proper funeral. ...
>
> While my sisters are trafficked and my brothers kidnapped.
> Every refugee wishes to go back home,
>
> ... I still shout for justice.
> All I want is to live again in my own home,
> A safe life, to enjoy my rights.
>
> The world I knew has gone,
> My people were killed and displaced.
> It's the fourth time I have fled Bangladesh,
> My life is spent just trying to survive.
>
> I always ask myself during repatriation:
> *"Is this the last time?"*
> *"Could I be fortunate enough to escape again?"*
> This time it is different. My heart is asking me. (Ali, p. 64)

The poet here expresses the Rohingya experience of alienation and chooses the 'strange land' over the land with which he associates his family history or his descent. The idea of dying in dignity is assured in the refugee camps rather than in the country that has treated his people as outsiders for decades. The right over his living and his dying is not ascertained by the 'owner' of the body but rather by the state that decides on whether the Rohingya man should be allowed to keep his life or to lose it. This experience can be further elucidated through the ideas propounded by Giorgio Agamben.

Giorgio Agamben, in his *Homo Sacer* propounds the idea of sacredness of life and the contradictory implications of the figure, *homo sacer*. This 'sacred man' is a man who is judged as a criminal, and sacrificing this man is not permissible yet a person who kills him is not condemned for murder either. In the context of a man (or society) who is discriminated against, his existence is a crime; and while the 'sacredness of life' is recognized widely, the act of killing him, is rendered unpunishable. (Agamben, p. 47) The sacred man, he further explains is both consecrated and damnable (Agamben uses the term 'taboo'), revered and evokes "horror". If *homo sacer* is either taboo or holy, then anyone who kills him is either contaminating himself or committing "sacrilege". The theory of the 'ambivalence of sacredness' which explains the duality of exclusion from both being sacrificed and the act of killing going unpunished is a "double exception...both from the sphere of the profane and from that of the religious" (p. 52). There is a pre-existence of 'political structure' with regard to the 'sacratio' or the consecrated; this structure exists prior to the "distinction between sacred and profane, religious and juridical" (p. 48).

Agamben critiques on Foucault's "biopolitics" that is simply explained as the politicization of bare life. Foucault explains that "the fundamental categorical pair" in western politics or perhaps world politics is not friend/enemy, but rather bare life/political existence, exclusion/inclusion. Man is a being, who "separates and opposes himself to his own bare life"; his life is defined by his inclusion in the mechanisms of state power and his "existence as a living being" (pp. 10, 12). Agamben expounds that the realm of 'bare life' would gradually coincide into the political realm so that the distinction between them becomes irreducible, and 'bare life' becomes the foundation in which the whole political system is rested (p. 12). When these distinctions are blurred, the bare life becomes "subject and object of the conflicts of the political power". In this sphere of political organization, there can emerge a system in which state power creates a living being who becomes the state's own object, or a democratic system in which the living being becomes a subject of political power. He explains that totalitarianism "transformed the decision on bare life into the supreme political principle." Behind democracy and its provision for recognition of rights and liberties, on the other hand, is the bare life, that can never be sacrificed but can yet be killed. Therefore, there is an "inner solidarity" between both extreme systems of political power (p. 13). Mayyu Ali's poem can be read through the lens of Agamben's *Homo Sacer* in the sense that a Rohingya man has become a subject and object of conflict surrounding his existence so that his life is not his own any longer. And thus he feels that it is better for him to die in the camps rather than for his "bare life" to coincide into the political realm of the state that oppresses him and his kind. This is expressed in the lines "My life is spent just trying to survive/I always ask myself during repatriation/Is this the last time?" (Ali, p. 64) The poems by Zaki Ovais and Ro Mehrooz can also be read through this theory of bare life by Agamben, apart from the other ways of extensive interpretation that are mentioned later on in this chapter.

Zaki Ovais, in his work entitled "Someone I'm afraid Of" identifies existence with inanimate elements of Nature. The stars, the fish, the river water, are few amongst the elements he personifies. The poem runs in the following lines:

> I'm a hungry star in the sky,
> covered by jealous clouds.
> I'm a goldfish plant in the garden,
> shaded from daylight.
> I'm a fly in the kitchen,
> Buzzing on the boundary of a blind wall.
> I'm a chicken under mother's wing,
> confined to the narrows of a wattle.
> I'm a dove on the street of Yangon,
> jailed in the cage of inhumanity.
> I'm the water flowing in Mayu river,
> missing my partner – Air.
> I'm a human in the universe,
> denied the most basic rights.
> I'm someone I'm afraid of. (Ovais, p. 33)

Interpreters of existential writers like Sartre and Camus are of the opinion that alienation is the umbrella in which all powerful writings of human suffering come under. In the essay, *Alienation and Existentialism in relation to Literature and Youth*, Henry Winthrop distinguishes Alienation into certain forms, two of which are "alienation from oneself" and "the alienation of man from society". The former, he explains, is an "interruption" that a person suffers whilst in the process of finding himself or in his words "quest for identity". In works of literature, when a character's development experiences a twist because of the interruption of harsh and unexpected circumstances, herein occurs an "alienation from oneself" (p. 290). In the line "I'm someone I'm afraid of", the speaker or the poet persona perhaps infers to this form of alienation. The latter form of alienation is that which alienates a person from a predominant society or culture. The first seed of social reform and change exists when a person suffers from such predicament. In keeping with the view of reform through writing, this form of alienation that pierces through in the comparison of the poet to the dove caged amidst the fastness of life in a busy street is in itself a loud voicing of the inhumanity around him.

Ro Mehrooz, in his poem, "Broken Mirror" speaks of trauma and anxiety in the imagery of "the speaking mirror". The stanzas tell the reader of fear and frustration the narrator feels in looking at the reflection of one's own countenance; and having that same reflection looking back at the narrator or the person. The poet speaks of the lack of recognition of the self that is reflected in a mirror. His trauma has made him incapable of recognizing the self that he thought he knew.

Jacques Lacan in his work *The Mirror Stage as Formative of the function of the I as Revealed in Psychoanalytic Experience*, speaks of a stage of development of the human psyche in which "identification" takes place, whereby a certain amount of change takes place in a person "when he assumes an image". Lacan explains, "…the *I* is precipitated in a primordial form, before it is objectified in the dialectic of identification with the other, and before language restores to it, in the universal, its function as subject" (Lacan, p. 1165) which is to say that the *I* depended its existence on the *other* without knowing the difference between the *other* and the self, in the initial stage of development of the human psyche; but with the intervening of language, this distinction becomes clear to the *subject* or self. Lacan explains that the image that the *subject* sees in the mirror is a cusp for seeing the "visible world" and that the *imago* (Latin for likeness or statue), which is perhaps the image of the subject presented in a mirror, represents or infers "hallucinations or dreams"; things that transcend the physical reality, things that are illusions which may "concern individual features…its infirmities..." but more importantly, the appearance of a "double" through which psychological reality is represented in the mirror reflection (p. 1166).

The inner world/outer world aspect of the mirror stage elucidates more clearly as far as the idea of the identity crisis of the self or the *I* is concerned. There is an establishment of a relationship between the *I* and the outside reality which is the outside of an 'organism' or outside the self; and the *I* that has a relation with the inner reality, a world which only exists within or in the innermost depths of the psyche or consciousness. Lacan describes the transitioning of the *I* in the mirror stage from having "caught up in the lure of spatial identification" to the time when the *I* becomes clothed in "the armour of an alienating identity" (p. 1167). He states that there is a conflicting nature in the relationship of the image and of the self. Thus, there is a tension between the subject and the image as the complete nature of the image, threatens the self of disintegration. The division in the *I* or the lack of unity in the self, paves way for a desire for the self to resolve into becoming whole.

In the first two stanzas Mehrooz's poem can be interpreted as the narrator describing the *imago* as the "speaking mirror" and the "disintegrated self" that does not "dare to look/at the mirror, looking/ at the mirror looking back" which perhaps could be because of the conflict between the narrator and the image; the conflict could be in the differences of each of their perception of realities. An outside force disturbs these events in the self or the *I* as "the bullet flew towards my head". The outer world or outside reality intervenes to exterminate the self which is the narrator, and the self in a quick moment of self-preservation "ducked down and ran". Consider the following lines –

> The bullet smashes the mirror,
> Shards scatter over the floor.
> (Breathe-)
>
> *
>
> Today, I see the mirror
> In the taxi window
> In the barber's shop

These profound lines speak of the climactic but also touch upon the anti-climactic situations that the poet paints. There is a massive exasperation from being saved from death in the bullet hitting the mirror until pieces of the glass scatter dramatically all over the floor. The word "breathe" though in parenthesis, is a reference to self-assurance and speaking to the inner self or to assure the inner world of the *I* of its life or existence. In the last stanza, there is a very mundane tone, wherein the narrator says he sees the mirror, it could be the same mirror that broke; it could be any other mirror "in the taxi window/In the barber's shop". Perhaps the same cycle of thought could repeat in his viewing of his image, but for now, the Self unites and questions no longer what that scattered image over the floor is. That is the image that he has come into resolution that he must accept – the identity of himself, a Rohingya.

These works can also be seen through the perspective of trauma theory. Here, a reference must be made to Cathy Caruth. A major trauma theorist, Cathy Caruth, in her introductory essay *Trauma and experience* explains that trauma is not a phenomenon that is understood for "unconscious meaning" the way a wish or dream is understood; rather it is literally a return or revival of an event against the will of the individual who has experienced it. This "literality" and "non-symbolic nature" of traumatic events or traumatic dreams and flashbacks is essential to the analysis of trauma. Caruth states, "The traumatized, we might say, carry an impossible history within them, or they become themselves the symptom of a history that they cannot entirely possess" (Caruth, p. 5). Through the theorist's description of the Freudian concept of trauma, it is pointed that trauma does not disappear from memory by the process of forgetting of what is a reality. There is an "inherent latency" of reality within the traumatic experience itself. The "historical power" of the trauma is not only released through the fact that the traumatic experience can be repeated after temporary forgetting, but in and through the "inherent latency" of forgetting, is it experienced, in the first place (p. 8). Trauma is not experienced in the very moment that it occurs, and its evidence is only traced "in connection with another place and another time". The history of trauma is a "referential" one, it can be understood by the "inaccessibility of its occurrence" and Freud explains that trauma has two things that are intertwined under it, that of history and personal truth. The "impact" of a traumatic event or experience lies solely in its location in the past, its "belatedness" and its presence outside the boundaries of place and time (pp. 8, 9). Caruth also says that psychoanalytic theory, after the struggles of World War I, "speaks its obscurest thoughts out of an intense and not fully assimilated confrontation with death". Trauma, however is not only a suffering that is repeated, but is also a process of continual leaving "from its site" (p. 10). Theorists have suggested that isolation is a factor that is inextricably linked to trauma. Isolation is "imposed" by a traumatic event, although this is not an individual isolation but rather a historical one, the latter being "communicated at the level of our cultures". This communication or "listening of another" aids in helping to pass through the trauma; it is exemplified in the communication between the Hiroshima survivors and the Americans through a narrative written by Hersey and in general when survivors interact with other survivors. This process of speaking and listening, "from the site of trauma" does not depend on how much people know about each other, rather it depends on how much of their traumatic pasts is known. Thus, it is concluded that the link between cultures is not through an understanding of the pasts but the traumas from within the history of those cultures and "listen through the departures we have all taken from ourselves" (p. 11).

In all of the discussed poems, it is observed that although the subject matter of Rohingya poetry is exclusive to the experience of the refugees, thematically, the poems are universal. In recent times, poets from the camps have bonded over underground poetry reading sessions through forms of technology with Burmese poets who support the cause of the Rohingyas. The Rohingya conflict is one that has been exacerbated by mechanisms that are condoned by the state and thus the cause of the Rohingya people can only be supported by people living outside Myanmar than inside it. The unity of poets during periods of social chaos dates back to the time when poetry flourished during the colonial era according to Saungkha (2019). In contemporary times though, because of the military crackdown, poets cannot talk about Myanmar politics directly. In a conversation between Mayyu Ali and James Byrne, Ali speaks of the writing environment that he is in, he says, "…Writing about being a Rohingya in such a situation is a battle between trying to survive and raising the voices of people who are counted as forgotten in the world…" (p. 74) Writing in the English language comes with the purpose of a desire for the world to understand the plight of his people. When asked about the future of Rohingya poetry, Ali says that the ambition of Rohingya poets is to indulge in inspirational themes that create a hope for "reconciliation and togetherness" "inspiration to move forward" and to ultimately be able to bring communities to see eye to eye despite the on-going conflict between these communities.

REFERENCES

Agamben, Giorgio, (1998). *Homo Sacer Sovereign Power and Bare Life* translated by Daniel Heller-Roazen, Stanford University Press, Stanford, California.

Atrocities in Mayanmar. *Religion and Ethics Weekly,* April 18, 2014. https://www.pbs.org/wnet/religionandethics/2014/04/18/april-18-2014-atrocities-in-myanmar/22768/. Accessed 15 October, 2019.

Bhabha, Homi, (1992). The world and the home, *Social Text, No. 31/32, Third World and Post-Colonial Issue, pp. 141-153*, https://www/jstor.org/stable/466222. Accessed 25 October, 2019.

Byrne, James. Rohingya Writing as Activism: A conversation with Mayyu Ali, *World Literature Today*, https://www.worldliteraturetoday.org/2019/spring/rohingya-writing-activism-conversation-mayyu-ali-james-byrne. Accessed 7 October, 2019.

Foucault, Michel, *Society Must be Defended, Lectures at the College de France* 1975-1976 translated by David Macey, Picador, New York (pp. 239-263).

Hoffstaedter, Gerhard. *The Dominant Discourses of Refugees, Recognition, and Othering in Malaysia: Regimes of Truth versus the Lived Reality of Everyday Lifeespace.library.uq.edu.au › view › UQ693214_OA*

I am a Rohingya Poetry from the Camps and beyond; edited and introduced by James Byrne and Shehzaar Doja, Arc Publications, 2019.

Lacan, Jacques. The Mirror Stage as Formative of the Function of the I as Revealed in Psychoanalytic Experience; *The Norton Anthology of Theory and Criticism*, edited by Vincent B. Leitch, George Lynn Cross, Paul and Carol Daube, 2nd ed., pp. 1164-1167.

Lacan: The mirror stage Overview http://www.english.hawaii.edu/criticalink/lacan/. Accessed 10 October, 2019.

Lauzon, Claudette. Introduction: Unmaking Home, *The Unmaking of Home in Contemporary Art,* https://www.jstor.org/stable/10.3138/j.ctt1whm8v6.5. Accessed 25 October, 2019.

Milko, Victoria; Hammond, Clare. In Myanmar, underground poetry nights build bridges between Rohingya and Burmese writers. *Global Post,* October 01, 2019, https://www.pri.org/stories/2019-10-01/myanmar-underground-poetry-nights-build-bridges-between-rohingya-and-burmese. Accessed 8 October, 2019.

Powell, John. Us vs them: the sinister techniques of 'Othering'- and how to avoid them https://www.theguardian.com/inequality/2017/nov/08/us-vs-them-the-sinister-techniques-of-othering-and-how-to-avoid-them. Accessed 7 October, 2019.

Trauma explorations in Memory edited with introductions by Cathy Caruth, John Hopkins University Press published 1995.

Tun Khin Interviews with Al Jazeera on Two Child Policy in Arakan. *RB News*, May 26, 2013, http://www.rohingyablogger.com/2013/05/tun-khin-interviews-with-al-jazeera-on.html. Accessed 9 October, 2019.

Winthrop, Henry. Alienation and Existentialism in relation to Literature and Youth, *The Journal of General Education,* Vol. 18, No. 4 (January 1967), pp. 289-298, https://www.jstor.org/stable/27796044. Accessed 25 October, 2019.

Zarni, Maung. Hitler/Nazi Symbols are popular in Myanmar and now Mein Kampf is made accessible in Burmese. *RB Analysis*, September 25, 2017, http://www.rohingyablogger.com/2017/09/hitlernazi-symbols-are-popular-in.html. Accessed 8 October, 2019.

https://www.facebook.com/181431105572618/posts/i-was-a-refugee-no-one-wanted-by-saiful-rohin/1116256862090033/

Section II

4
Gender and Conflict

Sukalpa Bhattacharjee

In the context of gender and conflict, it is important to reimagine issues of women's security and mainstream discourses of peace and violence. A greater imperative is to redeem women's stereotypical image as a victim of conflict situations and to recast her as an actor whose agency is constituted and reconstituted during and after conflict situations. In order to do this one would have to generate a critique of social patriarchy which produces 'hegemonic masculinity' that impinge on women rights and agency. "Hegemonic masculinity" builds on the patriarchal gender order and ideology and legitimizes stereotyping of gender roles. "Hegemonic masculinity can be defined as the configuration of gender practice which embodies the currently accepted answer to the problem of the legitimacy of patriarchy, which guarantees (or is taken to guarantee) the dominant position of men and the subordination of women" (Connell, 1995, p. 77). The reconceptualization of gender as a relational category and gender studies' stronger engagement with feminist concerns with power has paved the way for gender and masculinity to become a useful tool for analyzing conflict. Of course, gender rivalry in everyday life itself operates as a more complex and more contradictory process in comparison to other social and political conflicts.

Conflict from the social point of view refers to the struggles between two parties over scarce resources and goals that are not compatible. In the same vein, from the political perspective, conflict may be seen as intensified struggle at any level among groups who have the aim of gaining influence in areas of "power, resources, interest, needs" and to a certain degree, one of the group presupposes that there is incompatibility in that dimension of relationship (Igbuzo, 2011, p. 1). In the context of gender, conflict mostly springs from women's contestation of stereotypes created by social patriarchy. Gender violence is understood as violence targeted at groups and individuals on the basis of their gender. Violence therefore emanates from the presumed stereotypes of roles of men and women that are constructed by society and culture, legitimized through various agencies of power and circulated through false narratives and myths about capabilities of men and women by patriarchal institutions. Patriarchy is a form of mental, social, spiritual, economic and political organization/ structuring of society produced by the gradual institutionalization of sex-based political relations created, maintained and reinforced by different institutions linked closely together to achieve consensus on the lesser value of women. Most forms of feminism characterize patriarchy as a present day unjust social system that subordinates, discriminates or is oppressive to women. Many countries have endured decades of armed conflict, and others live under the permanent menace of political violence. Throughout, the gendered impacts of armed conflict and political violence are key issues which remain unresolved. The gendered causes, costs, and consequences of violent conflicts have been underrepresented, and often misrepresented (Moser & Clark, 2002, p. 230).

Conflict involving arms is a ubiquitous phenomenon. Since the dawn of the 21st century, armed conflicts have become more internal, long-drawn, and complex, with civilians increasingly becoming the targets (Bennet *et al.*, 1995). Armed conflicts affect both men and women, but their respective experiences may differ, at times significantly. Traditionally, women are not seen as combatants; though history does bear witness to women combatants, as in Sri Lanka and Liberia, the majority of soldiers continue to be men. Men may also be victims of violence, even sexual, in an armed conflict. Women, however, form the highest proportion of adult civilian population who get killed and targeted for abuse in war and they also suffer physical, economic, and psychological abuse (*Amnesty International USA,* 2010, p. 2).While conflict affects both men and women, women experience the consequences of conflict more acutely because of the nature of violence experienced by them through their bodies. They may get directly targeted for rape, molestation, and torture; they may also suffer indirectly by being related to men. Consequences of conflict, war and other hyper masculinities are mostly inscribed on the bodies of women, making bodies of women the crucial sites where violent histories are written. Apart from direct effect of conflicts and war the indirect sufferings of women in armed conflict are usually long-term, invisible, and often not acknowledged. For the women in many communities, the loss of their men often means losing their main breadwinner, leading a life with an uncertain future, and raising the household in the atmosphere of fear and social ostracism. As a consequence, women may get pushed into public spheres and male-dominated arenas. But, this 'gender mainstreaming' may not necessarily get reflected in their gaining decision-making powers both within and outside their homes. Often, post-conflict, women are expected to revert to their 'women' chores, even when they may have transcended the traditional boundaries during the conflict (Farr, 2009, p. 327). Again, as Sjoberg and Peet assert, "When feminists argue that 'men' protect 'women' in war, they mean that 'masculinity' protects 'femininity' ideationally, whether or not men (or anyone else) protects women (or anyone else) in real material terms." (Sjoberg, 2011, p. 167). This is how violence is legitimized through a relationship established between violence, citizenship, and hegemonic masculinity, so that all depend upon each other for permanence and recreation. "Women's need for protection justifies wars, but it also justifies the social dominance of masculinity, a requirement for war-fighting ..." (Confortini, 2006, p. 333). Leatherman (Leatherman, 2011, p. 41) posits the concept of a "runaway norm" that permits the shattering of traditional limits on violence and the legitimizing of crossing of several types of limits with regard to "the type of violence and "the intended targets of violence". Hypermasculinity and warring masculinities create insecurities for women particularly in cases of physical dislocation. As Leatherman notes, "the bodies of women, girls, and sometimes men may be the last lootable goods" (156).

One of the most glaring cases in the light of the issues argued above is the Kashmir conflict in India and its effect on the lives of women. The conflict in Jammu & Kashmir has been going on since the 1920s at diverse levels and with continuous variation of its nature since armed insurgency began in the region. Both directly and indirectly, their sufferings have been manifold. They have faced harassment from both the armed forces, as a punishment for their support to the armed struggle and also to 'break' the movement and the militant groups, who wanted to reinforce hegemony in the region or punished them for being state informers (Qutab, 2012, p. 256). Along with attacks on their life and safety, they were specifically targeted for rape and abuse. In most societies, 'honour' is directly associated with its women and this is true for the Kashmiri society as well. There is an angry outburst when women's honour, which is mostly associated with the Victorian ideas of virginity and chastity, is violated. But a culture fed with patriarchal values often fails to support the women victims or understand the violation of her bodily integrity or sense of dignity. As mentioned earlier, in some cases, women may not be the direct targets of the violence, yet their sufferings will be severe and long drawn. This happens often with the death, disappearance, or disability of the male member, whereby the women are left to struggle for survival on their own, or made to suffer for the actions of men. As a result, many women are forced to venture out of homes in search for remunerative work and so they also face harassment by armed forces. Even now, many such women who are left behind in the armed conflict as survivors lead an invisible existence in suffering and neglect. In Kashmir, the killings and disappearances of men have left behind a large number of women struggling for survival. It is estimated that there are some 20,000 widows of the armed conflict, many of whom are very young. The conflict-hit society was unprepared to meet the staggering numbers of widows who still face apathy at many quarters. Relatives often refuse to support them and they bear the burden of raising children alone (Kazi, 2009). They are often illiterate and have little or no knowledge of their rights and entitlements. The first difficulties surface soon after the death of their partners, in the forms of emotional stress, denial of inheritance rights, sexual harassment and general social ostracization. This is compounded by the difficulties that arise gradually, such as loss of control over the children, and a growing sense of despair. Finally, the widows are burdened by the long-term and growing demands of house care and the assignment of menial responsibilities. Altogether, the women find their position thoroughly compromised (Bukhari, 2002, p. 41).

But, besides the increasing number of widows, the armed conflict has also given rise to many 'half-widows'. These are women whose husbands have 'disappeared' or are missing in the conflict and often presumed dead, even though there is no proof of their death. It is estimated that there are at least 1,000 half widows in the valley (Anjum, 2007, p. 6) even though there has been no survey till date to estimate the exact numbers. The status and identity of half widows is a peculiar predicament. They are neither recognized socially as wives or as widows. Half-widows experience many of the same problems as widows, but their situation bears some unique aspects such as uncertainty about the existence of their loved one or official recognition of their status as an in-between of a wife and a widow since there is no proof of thc husband's death. The struggle for survival with the sudden loss of the main breadwinner often pushes them to poverty and suffering. These women neither find social rehabilitation nor get justice for their loss and so their life is wasted negotiating at various official and unofficial levels in search of their missing spouse and seek justice.

However, one observes that the image of women and/in war and conflict literature posit women as victims rather than as active actors, largely as a result of patriarchal structures. Women in fact occupy a number of roles and create different fates for themselves, as war is also a site of potential change. Women are seldom integrated within processes of peace negotiations from the very outset. An analysis of women's roles and the inclusion of women working in conflict situations reveal that women are not only fighters and/or victims, but also negotiators in post-conflict futures. A critical examination of women's participation in formal and informal peace-building activities shows that in most cases women are excluded from formal peace negotiations. Such high-level negotiations are identified as male domains (Gardam & Charlesworth, 2000, p. 148), which means that they also employ discourses and practices that are closer to men's reality than to women's. As a result, women also lack direct influence in the identification of reconstruction priorities that are usually part of a peace agreement. Nevertheless, women are demonstrated to play an influential role through their work in grassroots organizations working for peace and reconciliation. From within these organizations, women constantly challenge the authorities and other members of society with demands for peace, non-discrimination, accountability, recognition of human rights, etc. While always positioned on the margins, these organizations show their ability to mobilize large numbers of women, and to translate individual grievances into legitimate social concerns. Moreover, many of them play a significant role in building a new culture of peace at the local level by organizing peace education and community-based reconciliation and social reconstruction activities.

In a post-war situation, the end of war does not signal the end of violations against women. Often many women confront more discrimination in reconstruction programs, sexual and domestic violence in refugee camps, and violence when they attempt to return to their homes. It is reported that in Afghanistan, women of all ethnicities have been compelled to restrict their participation in public life even after the fall of the Taliban to avoid being 'targets of violence by armed factions and those seeking to enforce repressive Taliban-era edicts' (Ingushetia, 2000). Again Afghan women, especially those living outside Kabul, continue to face serious threats to their physical safety, denying them the opportunity to exercise their basic human rights and to participate fully and effectively in rebuilding their country. Also in Iraq, insecurity and fear of sexual violence and abduction are keeping women in their homes and out of schools or away from work. Despite being on such vulnerable margins, women have been able to constitute various subjectivities to transform their vulnerability into creative agencies for encounter and redemption.

Therefore, our understanding of women's roles in post-war societies and of their contributions to post-war reconstruction must go beyond the universalistic narrative of "women's experience of war" and their vulnerability. The specificity and diversity of women's experiences must be acknowledged. Only on this basis can we conduct comparative analyses and begin to develop a deeper general understanding of post-war reconstruction from a gender perspective. Such a perspective would involve a shift in the representation of the image of women from vulnerable victims to an image of women as a highly differentiated group of social actors, who possess valuable resources and capacities and who have their own agendas. Women influence the course of things, and their actions are constitutive of post-war societies. The reduction of women to targets and beneficiaries both fails to recognize their contributions and therefore results in their marginalization.

There is also a need for gender-specific data and gender-focused analysis in order to see women's situation within a gender framework which pays attention to how gender roles and relationships are continuously constructed and contested by different actors, and which recognizes the gender dimension inherent in all aspects of war and post-war reconstruction. The gender perspective is also relevant for the achievement of sustainable peace. If peace is a structure of expectations based on specific balance of powers, the failure to recognize gender issues may produce new social tensions and contribute to the differentiating struggles over identity, status and power that are so distinctive for societies which have recently achieved peace. Although women wage peace in conflict situations, reports and studies on the effects of armed conflict tend to incorporate women in the general category of civilians without siting or citing the differences in gendered experience of violence. As already mentioned, on the one hand as members of the civilian population women experience distinctive economic problems in armed conflict. In many cases, women are separated from the men who traditionally may be their source of income. Many cultural factors exacerbate the economic problems already faced by women. Women are forced to leave their homes or are forced to evacuate when war or conflicts break out. In the process they are exposed to foreign conditions which render them more vulnerable to accidents, injuries and rape. This is also a basic dislocation from physical and reproductive health. Further, as internally displaced persons and refugees, women are mistreated in camps and new countries. Mention may also be made of the Sri Lankan situation where according to Darini Rajasingham-Senanayake, "During two decades of armed conflict in north-east Sri Lanka, women have carved new spaces of agency and new roles as armed combatants, principal income generators or heads of household in the absence of menfolk. Will they be pushed back 'into the kitchen' with a return to peace, also often indexed as a return to the pre-war gender status quo?" (Rajasingham-Senanayake, 2004, p. 141). A similar phenomenon can also be studied in the context of political conflict in Nepal where women on the one hand are suffering tremendous physical and psychological displacement and on the other hand are trying to negotiate between warring parties in an alternative civic space (Sarup, 2005).

Women in conflict situations do not represent the official voices of war such as the government or the military. Therefore, they are non-state actors who exist off-stage but who help either to further a war or critically challenge it. One knows how women have historically served the war process by providing the day to day maintenance of war on the one hand and relinquishing male children to the 'cause' on the other. Studies have been conducted to show how women have served as pawns in conflict and war situations through systematic rape, forced prostitution etc. (Leathy, 1997, p.15). At the same time, women as non-state actors have also served as voices of resistance. What is significant in the role of Women's groups and organizations in conflict situations, is that they are powerful agents of what Swanee Hunt calls "Inclusive Security" which she says "rests on the principle that fundamental social changes are necessary to prevent renewed hostilities" (Hunt, 2001, p. 41). Conflict does not get resolved by signing peace accords and women in post-conflict situation have always worked at the grass roots levels to affect social change. Women execute this role by collaborative approach to governmental agencies and dominant diplomatic structures thereby enlarging the civic space for citizen-empowerment. Social change that would 'prevent renewed hostilities' can also be affected through the articulation of alternative narratives of physical and spiritual sufferings of human beings in a conflict situation as against the male-centred universalist narratives of war and conflict.

Therefore, a very effective means of participation of women has been their attempt to creatively narrate the lives of various women in conflict situations and sometimes to also write of one's own self. Rigoberta Menchú Tum is the subject of the testimonial biography *I, Rigoberta Menchú* (1983) and the author of the autobiographical work, *Crossing Borders.* Similarly, former US Ambassador Swanee Hunt vividly chronicles the experiences of twenty-six Bosnian women in her book *This Was Not Our War.* The women share riveting descriptions of their wartime experiences as well as their heartfelt and courageous efforts to repair the wounds inflicted upon their neighbours and their country. Ambassador Hunt became involved in diplomatic and humanitarian efforts in the war-torn former Yugoslavia while serving as the US Ambassador to Austria in the 1990s. Hunt interviewed each woman several times over the course of seven years, skilfully weaving their experiences into a startling narrative of what life was like during this chaotic and terrifying time. Spanning all ethnic groups and heritages, the accounts of these women – politicians, doctors, journalists, businesswomen, and mothers – offer the reader the diverse reasons for the war. Their dramatic stories chronicle daily survival in the war zone and describe their hopes as peace returns and healing begins due in large part due to their efforts. The women describe the heartbreak of watching their multicultural society disintegrate into chaos and violence while senior politicians manipulate the country into an unwanted war. They witness wartime atrocities that include rapes of neighbours and friends, daily survival in the crossfires of a sniper's rifle and camps where husbands, sons and brothers disappeared, some never to be seen or heard from again. The accounts of the violence and the struggle to survive are at times hard to bear, but with the introduction of the Dayton Peace Agreement and the prospect of peace, they begin to look toward the future and their stories become hopeful. Instead of succumbing to self-pity or hatred, each woman takes action to implement change and improve the conditions for those around them. These stories of courage, imagination, initiative and forgiveness are inspiring and emotional: one woman founding an organization to help war survivors cope with post-traumatic stress disorder, another helping survivors find and repair their damaged homes, and a third starting a community art project to raise funds for women's causes that also helps survivors' healing through art therapy. Mention may also be made in this context of an article by Hanna Herzog where she analyses the way the marginality of Israeli-Arabs in general and women in particular within Israeli society trickles down into women's peace organizations, and how structures shape feminine and civil identity. Contextualizing women's narrative and rendering their cultural and historical specificity illuminates the singularity of their social position, which shapes a different feminist voice – one that is openly defiant toward the Jewish society but is also critical of its own community. Their location on the periphery of various social categories – citizenship, gender, national and local-community belonging – that demarcate the boundaries of identity and social affiliation results in multiple voices and solutions. This study by Hanna Herzog is based on fifty in-depth interviews conducted in 1995 with Palestinian-Israeli women who were members of various peace organizations. Similarly, making a critique of a technocratic and masculine concept of 'national security' Urvashi Butalia has edited a volume entitled *Speaking Peace: Women's Voices from Kashmir* (Butalia, 2002) which looks into the gendered impact of violence on the women of Kashmir, their living environments, health, eating habits, their work and workplaces, their access to education and so on. Yet not much is being written about their response to the conflict. The volume documents the experiences of a wide range of women in coping with the impact of the conflict on their lives and raises relevant questions regarding their coping strategies and the options before them. Interviews with Kashmiri women, personal reflective pieces, excerpts from various reports and books, a photo essay, journalistic dispatches and a socialistic excerpt on the rights and privileges promised to women in the *Naya Kashmir Manifesto* adopted by the National Conference in 1984 are among the contents of the volume.

An extremely significant feature of women's voice from South-Asia in general and South-east Asia in particular and the countries discussed above is that women across the globe are trying to resist violence both in private and public spaces and ensuring 'feminized security perspectives'. The emphasis is not only on national security but transnational security as the common causes for women's sufferings particularly in South-Asia arise due to religious fundamentalism and communal ideologies. For example, a common source for the sufferings of the women of the Indian sub-continent is an aggressive nationalism leading to Partition (Dan, 2001, p. 128). This has been reiterated by several women's organizations in India and Pakistan like the Muslim women conference of 1986 and the Women's Action Forum (WAF) of 1981. Simorgh women's resource and publication centre which brought a great realization of commonality and common bondages between the women of India and Pakistan working foı the same cause collaborated with likeminded Indian women organizations and publication centres such as Kali for Women and Sakshi over several human rights and peace issues in late nineties.

Thus, a study of women in conflict situation involves a more nuanced assessment of their victimization in conflict situation and a subsequent construction of subjectivities on their part to create alternative spaces of post-conflict reconstruction. Interrogating the connection between women and peace has to be understood in the context of prevailing unequal power relations in the society. There is dire need to explore linkage between masculinity and violence. The patriarchal notion of security, peace and power cannot be, comprehending women's experiences, needs and responses. Rita Manchanda says, "The politics of rape are imbricated in women's bodies being a marker of community identity both as metaphor and a physical reality. Moreover, the targeting of women in any counter-insurgency is designed as of war to destroy community which women all through conflict continue to hold together" (Manchanda, 2001, p. 1956). The fourth world conference on women took bold initiative against sexual abuse and rape of women during war and violent conflict. It calls on states to take immediate steps with regard to ending the use of war related violence against women, thereby considering it as crime against humanity. The violence experienced by women in conflict situations, is in a continuum alongside the violence perpetrated on women in normal times. Women's experience of conflict is contextual and therefore cannot be fixed within a framework of analysis since women's support to peace, militarisation and war depends on unique particularities of conflict within different societies. There is a need to view women as not victims alone, but also as agents of social and cultural transformation through various agencies constituted by them. Women's peace activism and initiatives therefore cannot be and should not be underrepresented.

REFERENCES

Anjum, Aaliya. (2007). 'Wailing woes', Combat law, *The Human Rights Magazine*, *6* (5): 6-9.

Amnesty International USA (*AIUSA*) (2010). Violence against women in armed conflict: A factsheet, *www.amnestyusa.org/women/pdf/armedconflict.pdf* (accessed on 3 July, 2019).

Butalia, Urvashi (ed.) (2002). *Speaking Peace: Women's Voices from Kashmir*; Kali for Women.

Bukhari, Fayaz. (2002). Dying day by day, *Himal South Asian* (Kathmandu, Nepal: Himalmedia), *15*(11): 38-40.

Confortini, Catia. Galtung, (2006): Violence and Gender: The Case for a Peace Studies/Feminism Alliance. *Peace and Change,* 31, no. 3, 333-367.

Connell, Raewyn. (1995). *Masculinities.* Cambridge: Polity Press.

Del Zotto, Augusta C. (2002). Women, Wringing Hands: How the Mainstream Media Stereotyped Women's Experiences in Kosovo. *Journal of Gender Studies*, Vol. 11, No. 2, 2002, p. 141.

Dan, Inger Skjelsbæk. (2001). *Gender, Peace and Conflict*, London: SAGE. p. 128.

Farr, Vanessa, Henri Myrttinen and Albrecht Schnabel. (2009). Sexed pistols. *The Gendered impacts of small arms and light weapons*, New York: United Nations University Press.

Hunt, Swanee and Cristina Posa (2001). Women Waging Peace, *Foreign Policy,* No. 124, pp. 37-47.

Igbuzor, O. (2011). Peace and Security Education: A Critical Factor for Sustainable Peace and National Development, *International Journal of Peace and Development Studies*, *2*(1), 1-7.

Ingushetia, (2000). Peter Bouckaert/*Human Rights Watch http://hrw.org/ Women and Armed Conflict; International Justice.* Visited on 23rd July, 2019.

J. Gardam & H. Charlesworth. (2000). Protection of Women in Armed Conflict, *Human Rights Quarterly*, *22*, pp.148-166.

Kazi, Seema (2009). *Between democracy and nation: Gender and militarization in Kashmir*. New Delhi: Kali For Women.

Leatherman, Janie L. (2011). *Sexual Violence and Armed Conflict*, Malden, MA: Polity Press.

Leathy, M. (1997). *Conflict Through A Gendered Lens*, Paper presented at the Ist Annual Symposium on International Relations, Institute for Conflict Resolution, Brussels, pp. 15-17.

Manchanda, Rita (2001). Redefining and Feminising Security, *Economic and Political Weekly*, June 2-8, Vol. 36, No. 22, pp. 1956-1963.

Moser, Caroline O.N. and Fiona C. Clark. (2002). Victims, Perpetrators or Actors? Gender, Armed Conflict and Political Violence, *Development in Practice* , Vol. 12, No. 2 (May, 2002), pp. 230-232.

Olivia, Bennett, Jo Bexley and Kitty Warnock (1995). *Arms to fight, arms to protect: Women speak out about conflict*. London: Panos Publications.

Qutab, Soudiya, Women Victims of Armed Conflict: Half-widows in Jammu and Kashmir, *Sociological Bulletin*, May-August 2012, Vol. 61, No. 2 (May-August 2012), pp. 255-278.

Rajasingham-Senanayake, Darini.(2004). Between Reality and Representation. *Cultural Dynamics*, Vol. 16, No. 2-3, 141-168.

Sjoberg, Laura and Jessica Peet, (2011). A(nother) Dark Side of the Protection Racket, *International Feminist Journal of Politics,* 13, No. 2 (June 2011): 167.

Sarup, Kamala (2005). Women Trafficking and Conflict, *Scoop Independent News*. Monday, 14 March.

5

Re-Imagining the Catholic Imagination

Queer, Self and Conflict in Norman E. Pasaribu's *Sergius Seeks Bacchus*

Lede-e-miki Pohshna

In the *Mad Woman in the Attic*, Gilbert and Gubar point out that:

> Women from Jane Austen and Marry Shelly to Emily Bronte and Dickinson produced literary works that are in some sense palimpsestic, works whose surface designs conceal or obscure deeper, less accessible (and less socially acceptable) levels of meaning. Thus these authors managed the difficult task of achieving true female literary authority by simultaneously conforming to and subverting patriarchal literary standards (1979, p. 73).

Gilbert and Gubar argues that the hidden, obscure and unacceptable meanings serve as the palimpsest for female writer of the nineteenth century to work their material on (Dillon, 2007, p. 102). However, there are certain writings in which the palimpsest is not the "less accessible level of meaning" but in which the reverse of palimpsest theory of criticism is true. For instance, a popular, acceptable layer is used in order to create the unacceptable semantics. This reverse palimpsest demands a reimagination of a certain context within the anti-tradition which the author wants to work with/on. One such important work is *Sergius Seeks Bacchus* (2019) by Norman E. Pasaribu. It is a queer anthology that uses, appropriates, reimagines and reinterprets the catholic imagination in order to produce reverse-palimpsestic queer poems.

The term "Catholic Imagination" was popularised by Andrew Greely (Follman, 2010) and it refers to the catholic viewpoint of God's omnipresence in all creation as a whole. This imagination according to Runar Edelbo (2003) is "analogical" and which is "found in creation itself and views creation as God in disguise" (para. 4). On the origin of the Catholic Imagination, Flannery O' Connor observes:

> St Augustine wrote that the things of the world pour forth from God in a double way: intellectually into the minds of the angels and physically into the world of things. To the person who believes this – as the western world did up until a few centuries ago – this physical, sensible world is good because it proceeds from a divine source...when Joseph Conrad said that his aim as an artist was to render the highest possible justice to the visible universe, he was speaking with the novelist's surest instinct. The artist penetrates the concrete world in order to find at its depths the image of its source, the image of ultimate reality. (1961, p. 157).

Some of the aspects of the catholic imagination are community, salvation, hierarchy, sacred place, sacred desire, etc. (Simpson, 2002, p. 124). The catholic imagination has driven these aspects into various works of art. However more relevant to this chapter is Heartney's observation regarding the relationship between the sacramental imagination with that of "physically provocative works it seems to inspire" (2001, p. vii). The sexualization of the spiritual which many critics such as Paglia (1990) and Huffington (1996) delve into is influenced by the distinctive catholic imagination. Emphasis on carnality as a culturally subversive act is sacramental in nature and "posits the existence of a distinctly catholic consciousness in sensuality and sexuality" (Heartney, 2001, p. 7). This chapter will examine Pasaribu's *Sergius Seeks Bacchus* as a subversive literature, while influenced and informed by the catholic imagination, as it also seeks to reimagine it in an attempt to create a coherent story about one's sense of self. This is an attempt on the part of the artist to negotiate through the many facets of conflicts that he has to undergo while he is in search of his own identity.

In the very title of the anthology *Sergius Seeks Bacchus* (Hereafter cited as *Sergius*) the poet uses the figures of two catholic saints – Sergius and Bacchus – to stress not only on the queerness of these two saints but to indicate the closeted-ness of their Christian experience. The discourse on 'the closet' is very consequential in formulating the knowledge/power binary relationship between the closet and its subject. Eve Kosofsky Sedgwick's reading on the story of Esther and how that knowledge/power relation operates, is a milestone in theorising the closet (Sedgwick, 1990).

Theorising the closet is also inherently linked with theorising the conflict in the context of queer because the closet is immanent in allowing the subject position to navigate the external conflict. But at the same time, the closet is also very consequential in internalising the external conflict within the psyche of the subject position. In the poem "Love", the poet says:

> When the rain pays a visit
> and he's sitting at home
> he climbs up the stairs and into his room
>   to make sure there are no leaks
> between the ceiling and the sky. (Pasaribu, 2019, p. 10).

The persona's angst in this poem is inherently tied to his fear of being outed. His act of checking that there should be no "leaks" "between the ceiling and the sky" is his attempt to be in the closet. There exists an analogical parallelism between the anxiety of the "leaks" and the anxiety of being "outed" which the queer subjects seek to hide, solve, navigate and live through. The anguish of being out is immanent in this poem. Being out would make visible his status as a queer and consequently his queer body. The persona's struggle with this knowledge/power relation is governed, in a significant way, by his religion which he expresses, in the poem "He and the Tree":

> He sought forgiveness for his granddad, the palm oil
> Company's founder, for the whole clan, really, who'd spent
> Generations taking a carpenter for god's own son. (11)

"God's own son" here is a reference to Jesus and in extension to Christianity. The person seeks forgiveness for his Christian family who are inclined in their rejection of his sexuality. The tree in this poem is symbolic of the queer desire. But on further reading, the symbol of the tree is very much a product of the catholic imagination. The reference to the "god having three branch-like a tree" (Pasaribu, p.11) is a reference to the Holy Trinity. This God – specifically the catholic God, is very much like the tree. But the tree, in this poem has a queer desire, where his lover is being "ripped from the earth/for being 'too close to the foundation'" (Pasaribu, p.11). What the author attempts here is to queerify religion. His catholic imagination enables him to see the tree as the embodiment of divinity. But the tree, signifying queer, is a reflection of that divinity itself. Despite the fact that the Catholic church does not sanction homosexuality (Dempsey, 2008, p. 77: Curran *et al.,* 1998, p. 178), the poet's vision of a god that sanctifies queer marriage is a re-imagining of the catholic imagination. Here, the poet subverts the catholic imagination itself in his attempt to portray a post-gay future, where homosexuality is being normativised (Harris, 1997, p. 6). The catholic imagination enables the poet to have a vision of a tree (of life) but that tree is being queerified by his queer self. This is akin to what Nayyar called the "queerifying of hetorosexist space" (2007, p. 144) but in this poem, the concept of divinity itself is being queerified.

In another poem "Inferno", Pasaribu reimagines the inferno of Dante and instead of Dante's vision, Pasaribu sees his own closeted self and his quest for a coherent story as being the ultimate inferno. In the poem he says:

> What do you seek in this dark pit
> *Apart from your tear and chattering teeth*
> Here you are with your baby face
> *You're empty, there's nothing to you at all*
>
> (Pasaribu, 2019, p. 20).

The closet is referred to as a dark pit. These lines capture the angst and agony of the closet and the closeted body in place like Indonesia. While some theorists such as Seidman (2003) argue that the closet is an antiquated metaphor due to the growing acceptance of homosexuality, they are making this observation in the context of the developed countries. In Indonesia, however, homosexuality is still a taboo. Despite the lack of anti-homosexuality laws in Indonesia, the Indonesian government allows for its provincial government to bring out any law on the line of Islam and this leads to the formulation of anti-homosexuality law in the province of Aceh (BBC "No Place to Hide"). And despite the legality or its lack thereof, the social condition of Indonesia as informed and influenced by Islam and Christianity is very much against homosexuality. As such, Indonesia as a whole becomes a metaphorical closet, a spatial externality which is being compared to the "dark pit'. Being queer to both the main religions of Indonesia is incompatible with their idea of being pure. As such, "the Heaven they talk about is out of reach" (Pasaribu, 2019, p. 20). The closeted queer struggle is perfectly captured by those images that shape the catholic imagination. The inferno or the flaming hell of Dante is the closet where the queer is being asphyxiated. The dark pit or the abyss is the closet itself that sucks the Indonesian queer forever into its dark depths because coming out is not an option.

The poems in this anthology *Sergius Seeks Bacchus* problematises many of the ideas of the catholic imagination like the idea of community, salvation, redemption, the sexuality of Christ, etc. The poem "On a pair of Young Men in the Underground Car Park at FX Sudirman Mall", the poet describes the homosexual desires are furtive and forbidden. The lovers have to open their eyes while kissing to keep watch of the janitor. This sense of fear and terror at being found out is due to the fact that society and religion refuses to tolerate homosexuality. But more than outlining the problem of the queer body, the poet is interested in bringing out the contradictions within the Catholic imagination. He opines that what propels him into the arm of another man is driven by the same force that propels Sergius into the arms of Bacchus. He questions the sainthood of Augustine of Hippo. If Augustine who proudly proclaimed "Lord make me chaste but just not yet" is imagined as a saint, then his love for another man should not debar him from living a dignified life. He thus puts forward:

> The two young men even wondered sometimes
> Why they were the ones who had to show love
> Can bloom anywhere, even in the dark
> And that love growing in the dark is no less life giving.
>
> (Pasaribu, 2019, p. 47)

The interpretation of the nature of procreation and subverting the role of heterosexuality in it is a radical queer subversion of family as an institution. Homosexual love is as much life giving just as heterosexual love. But life giving should not be confused with life creating. Here the poet wants to stress on the nature of queer love and its all-encompassing dimensions which allows it to embrace one and all. When the Catholic Church stresses on the unnaturalness of homosexuality by linking it to its inability to give life, Pasaribu reinvents the idea of giving life and make it akin with "nurturing life", a notion which can be found in his other poem "He and the Tree".

A general sense of internalised phobia doesn't seem to be the fulcrum in Pasaribu's reimagination of the Catholic imagination. According to Tiffany Tsao (2019), Christian elements are:

> Reworked, reshaped, into new theologies—one's critical and questioning, one's hopeful and queer-affirming. New gospels for the queer community. Heavens where a Sergius and Bacchus can stroll the streets hand in hand in broad daylight, rather than confining their love to the subterranean carpark of a third-rate-and-therefore-relatively-deserted shopping mall (p. 84).

The poet's usage of the Christian elements stem from his quest to self. The poet is a Batak and a Christian living in the Muslim majority Indonesia and as such, he faces a double marginalisation. In the poem "Curriculum Vitae" he states, "Some of the neighbours forbade their kids from playing with him/and his brothers because his family was Batak and Christian" (2019, p. 56). As someone who exists at the periphery of the periphery, the poet is further marginalised by the fact that he was queer. So there exists multiplicities of identities for the subject position – that of a Batak, a Christian and a Queer. This conflict of identities within him prompts him to search for a stable anchor with which he could define himself. On being queer, he says:

> The first thing he learned at school, as he watched the girls
> During break, was that there was a girl inside him. He believed that
> When he grew up his penis would expire and his breast
> would sprout (2019, p. 56).

Further:

> His father punished him with beating. One day he eavesdropped
> On his parents – his father was worried because according to him

> Their firstborn son acted like a girl. He peered into the mirror,
> To the little girl inside. And he saw it was good. (2019, p. 56)

The notion that "it was good" is evocative of God's utterance after seeing his creation as can be found in the Bible (*New International Version*, Gen,1:1-14). When he peered into the mirror, he is peering not at his reflection but at that very girl that he came to realise as inhibiting in his body. So in constructing that image, he becomes god, the Great I am of Moses, the Jungian ultimate consciousness. It is at this point that he firmly establishes his identity and ties it with that of a queer. His differentiation of the self in the mirror stage and his ability to identity with the opposite gender and observes that it was good is a final dawn of the great consciousness upon him. However, that identification with the queer results in his further marginalisation in his own Batak community. Of this he says:

> Not long after he graduated from college, he discovered the rest Of the Batak community called him 'sibanci' behind his back. (Pasaribu, 2019, p. 57)

Being Queer is not only a taboo in Indonesia and Christianity. It is also a taboo within his own community. This multiplicity of not only identities but also oppressed and marginalised identities bring about a semblance of unhomeliness within him. Homi K. Bhabha (1992) and Lauzon (2016) have problematised the concept of home and meaning of unhomeliness; how the structures and the semantics revolving around the concept of home as being impermanence in today's reality of conflict, statelessness and oppressive factors of history are being formulated by many critics. Furthering the idea of impermanence and the destabilisation of home and family in the context of queer, Judith Halberstam in asking to 'forget the family' opines:

> Queer intervention into kinship studies have taken many forms: some call for new model of family (Butler's Antigone as a substitute for Oedipus, Weston's chosen families as a substitute for a blood bond); others call for a recognition of friendship ties as kinship; and still other scholars ask that we recognize the difference that gay and lesbian parents make to the very meaning of family. But

> few scholars call for an emphasis on family or a rejection of the family altogether. (2007, p. 317)

In the poem "Curriculum Vitae", the poet persona has to "ran away" (Pasaribu, 2019, p. 57) from home because he was rejected by his family. Homelessness among queer people has been an area of extensive study (Abramovich, 2016; Bateman, 2015; Ecker, 2016; Nicholl, 2009; Paradis, 2017). The discomfort of being queer in a heteronormative society is the main reason for the queer homelessness (Matthews *et al.*, 2019, p. 232). Of the queer youths' predicament, Ecker observes that:

> Homeless queer youth had poorer outcomes in relation to all other indices, including mental health issues, suicidal behaviours, substance use, sexual victimisation, sexual risk behaviour, physical victimisation, discrimination/stigma, and social relationship. (2016, p. 343)

The poem "Curriculum Vitae" is almost a coming of age of a gay youth growing up Batak and Christian in Indonesia. His many suicide attempts and depression is symptomatic of the journey of many queer youths. One example of this is Bobby Griffith (1963-1983) which figures prominently in the poem "Aubade". The life and death of Bobby Griffith as portrayed in the movie *Prayers for Bobby* is the context with which the poet argues that the future (heaven) would be much easier for the queer people:

> It's a new day,
> And fear is far behind. You know
> Life doesn't stop here. There will be no Bobby
> No more (Pasaribu, 2019, p. 33).

Being homeless and being rejected by one's family are prevalent queer oppressive experiences. Being rejected outright by home and by one's own people poses a problem for the poet persona. He was "other-ised" within his own community. He is confused when it comes to the question of defining his status within the larger scheme of identity. As such if being queer is akin to being the condemned soul, both within his community and within his religion, he has to find ways and means of negotiating and recreating a coherent story about himself. His quest for self then begins with the question of "who am I?" in this larger scheme of things and how to reconcile the contradictions of his queer subject position with the other subject positions that he comes to occupy. Re-imagining his faith and its sacramental imagination is a let out which enables him to arrive at a semblance of coherence between the multiplicity of conflicting identities that he comes to manifest – Batak, Indonesian, Queer and Catholic. In the poem "He and the Tree", he says:

> At the altar
> They would be joined together before god, who had three
> branches-like a tree—and their children would fill the lot,
> every
> Square inch, so that someday everyone who passed
> Would think a forest had sprung up in the city's heart.
> The man hugged the tree and the tree hugged the man.
>
> (Pasaribu, 2019, p. 11)

This poem ends in a positive note just like many of Pasaribu's poems. For instance, in the poem "Sergius Seeks Bacchus", he ends the poem with:

> It all feels. Hand in hand, you two will stroll the streets,
> Introducing one another to everyone you meet.
>
> (2019, p .12).

This poem brings about the sexuality of Christ but also queerifying it at the same time. This subversive interpretation of sexuality is being done in order to bring out the encompassing and tolerant nature of the Christ that the poet had come to accept. He says:

> You seek your beloved – he appeared to you in your cell,
> His body glowing silvered as he whispered, Endure
> For I will always watch over you. With him you'll rise
> Up to heaven and wonder at how familiar
> It all feels... (12)

The poet re-imagines the story of Sergius and Bacchus. These two saints, however, cease to be mere catholic saints but they have been rendered queer, and so is their love story. But more than that, the closeted-ness of the experience of Sergius and Bacchus is also evocative of the closeted-ness of the queer experience. Not only the figure of Bacchus and Sergius, but even Christ has been queerified. Here the lover is synonymous with Christ when he exclaims, "for I will always watch over you". These words are the same words spoken by Christ to his disciples before his ascent to heaven. In this poem, the two lovers also ascended to heaven and there, they find that their love could thrive. Heaven is not only for the heterosexuals but it is for anyone who is capable of loving enough. In another poem "Poetry", the poet persona makes a decision of coming out to his wife. He declares:

> Time to stop living a lie. Everything is
> Nothing but a show. And you're a bad actor
> With no script, trying to make her life your stage.
> Who's watching? Your folks – and empty seats.
> You stand in the spotlight, unfiltered, unpink,
> Performing an endless series of bad tricks…
> Time to tell what transpire in the dark
> Time to gesture toward what's remain (Pasaribu, pp. 13-14).

The persona's whole heterosexual experience is just a gesture, a series of performances to enact a social mask, which Carl Jung (1956) describes as "a kind of mask, designed on the one hand to make a definite impression upon others, and on the other to conceal the true nature of the individual" (p. 190). The poet persona's ability to encounter and to confront the reality of his being is the completion of his individuation, psychologically speaking, which Jung describes as "restoration and restoration" (p.197). This allows for the presentation of the self that is not contradicting with the inherent and true nature of the self (Hannah, 2001, p. 288; Wehr, 1987, p. 57). On a larger scale, this "recovery and restoration" of the self allows the subject to create a coherent story about one self and one way it could do that is through the re-interpretation of the mythos and the ethos. Pasaribu's revisioning of the catholic imagination is his attempt at this creation of grand narrative about his queer self. The poem "Aubade" talks about the new hope in the new life and in the new heaven, where "there will be no Bobby/no more" (Pasaribu, 33). The poem "Theophilus" is a re-imagining of the first and the second chapter of Genesis. The poem is an answer to the horrible cliché of "Adam and Eve; not Adam and Steve". The poem re-imagines God as a Friend who creates wonderful thing for a human being. After creating everything, the friend says:

'It's so deserted. I'm lonely'
The Friend was silent
You will never be with someone who loves you most
'Let there be someone else', said the Friend
And then there he was, a someone else – like the man
(Pasaribu, p. 52)

Instead of creating a woman as a companion for the friend, the God-Friend created a man as the ultimate companion. This radical interpretation of the story of Biblical creationism is one ways of the poet's persona attempt at reconciling his belief with his desires. The poem "Curriculum Vitae" ends with:

> He will grow old. You will grow old. Together you both will grow Old, and be wed before the Three-Branched-God-the-tree-like god-.
> And have a child named Langit. Your descendants will fill the earth
> So that whenever anyone is walking alone in the dark they will hear
> From every window in every building on both sides of the street,
> Voices reaching out , 'Salam!' 'Salam!'; Salam!'. (58).

The poem juxtaposes the Christian element of the Holy Trinity with the Islamic declamation of "Salam" or peace. This yearning for peace, for acceptance is the yearn of the queer folks to be accepted and to live a dignified life. Moreover, while the Christian God in popular imagination is being seen as intolerant to the idea of homosexual, the poet persona re-imagines this god to be an all accepting God, blessing and solemnising the union of two men in holy sacrament.

These poems portray the conflict of identities of a queer persona, while navigating through the multiplicity of identities that come to define him. The problem of navigating and managing multiple identities has been studied by many scholars (Stevens, 2004; Pietkiewicz, 2008). Pargament, Koenig and Perez (2000) have shown how contradicting belief systems can lead to distress within a subject position. In their study of queer Catholics and their reconciliation of their sexuality with their faith, Pietkiewicz and Kolodziejczyk in their 2016 paper opines that the queer folks "experienced at different moments of their lives intense conflict between developing sexual awareness and needs, and their religious beliefs and aspirations" (np). Internal conflict within the subject position poses the struggle or the attempt at achieving a sense of internal peace and this leads to the poet persona's re-imagination of his faith and the Catholic imagination. In as much as the Catholic imagination enables him to encompass the issue of divinity and its immanence in his art, his quest for identity and peace enables him to subvert and to reimagine the Catholic imagination itself.

REFERENCES

Abramovich, A. (2016). Preventing, reducing and lending LGBTQ youth homelessness: The need for targeted strategies. *Social Inclusion, 4*, 86-96.

Bateman, W. (2015). *LGBT youth homelessness: A UK national scoping of cause, prevalence, response and outcome*. Albert Kennedy Trust.

BBC (2017). No Place to Hide for LGBT People In Indonesia's Aceh Province. *BBC News,* 24 May, 2017. Web. 25 October, 2019. http://www.bbb.com/news/world-asia-40024204

Bhabha, Homi K. (1992). The world and the home. In *Third World and Post Colonial Issues*. 141-153.

Curran, Charles E., Charles A. Curran and Richard A. McCormick (1998). *John Paul II and Moral Theology*. Paulist Press.

Dempsey, Robert J. (2008). *The Linacre Quarterly*, Vol. 75. Catholic Medical Association.

Dillon, Sarah (2007). Queering the Palimpsest: H.D. in *The Palimpsest: Literature, criticism, theory* (Continuum Literary Studies, pp. 102-126). London: Continuum.

Ecker, J. (2016). Queer, young, and homeless: A review of the literature. *Child and Youth Service, 37*, 325-361.

Edelbo, Runar (2003). Roman Catholic imagination according to Andrew M. Greely. *Pietisen. 18*(2), Minneapolis.

Follman, Jeanne (2010). What is the Sacramental Imagination? *Aquinasblog,* February 4, 2010. *Aquinasblog* http://www.aquinasblog.com/2010/02/04/what-is-the-sacramental-imagination/

Gilbert, Sandra and Gubar, Susan (1979). *Mad woman in the attic: The women writer and the nineteenth century literary imagination*. Yale University Press.

Halberstam, Judith (2007). Forgetting family: Queer alternatives to Oedipal relations. In G.E. Haggerty and M. McGarry (Eds). *A Companion to LGBTQ Studies*, Blackwell, 315-24.

Hannah, Barbara (2001). *Striving towards wholeness*. Bloomsbury.

Harris, Daniel (1997). *The Fall and Rise of Gay Culture*. Ballantine Books.

Heartney, Eleanor (2004). *Post-modern heretics: The Catholic imagination in contemporary art*. Midmarch Press.

Huffington, Arianna (1996). *Picasso: Creator and Destroyer*. Simon and Schuster.

Jung, Carl G. (1956). *Two Essays on Analytical Psychology*. Routledge.

Lauzon, Claudette (2016). Introduction: Unmaking Home. *The Unmaking of Home in Contemporary Art*. University of Toronto Press.

Matthews, Peter, Christopher Poyner and Richard Kjellgren (2019). Lesbian, Gay, Bisexual, Transgender and Queer experiences of homelessness and identity: Insecurity and Home(o)normativity. *International Journal of Housing Policy*, *19*(2), 232-253.

Nayar, Pramod K. (2007). Queering culture studies: Notes towards a framework. *The Phobic and the Erotic: The Politics of Sexualities in Contemporary India*, edited by Brinda Bose and Subhabrata Battacharyya. Seagull, 118-148.

Nicholls, McNaughton (2009). Agency, transgression and the causation of homelessness: A contextualised national action analysis. *International Journal of Housing Policy*, *9*, 69-84.

O'Connor, Flannery (1961). Novelist and believer. *Mystery and Manners: Occasional Prose*. Farrar, Straus and Giroux, 154-168.

Paglia, Camille (1990). *Sexual Personae: Art and Decadence from Nefertiti to Emily Dickinson*. Yale University Press.

Pargament, K.I., Koening, H.G and M.L. Perez (2005). The many methods of religious coping: development and initial validation of the RCOPE. *Journal of Clinical Psychology*, *56*, 519-543

Pietkiewicz, I. (2008). Culture, *Religion and Ethnomedicine: The Tibetan Diaspora in India*. University Press of America.

Pietkiewicz, I. and M. Kolodziejczyk-Skrzypek (2016). Living in sin? how gay Catholics manage their conflicting sexual and religious identities. *Sexual Behaviour*, *45*(6). 1573-85.

Paradis, E. (2017). Why is the issue of LGBTQI homelessness still visible?. *Homeless in Europe Magazine: LGBTIQ homelessness*, Autumn.

Pasaribu, Norman E. (2019). *Sergius Seeks Bacchus*. Translated by Tiffany Tsao, Tilted Axis Press.

Sedgwick, Eve K. (1990). *Epistemology of the closet*. University of California Press.

Seidman, Steven (2003). *Beyond the Closet: The Transformation of Gay and Lesbian Life*. Routledge.

Simpson, John H. (2002). Review of the catholic imagination by Andrew Greeley. *Sociology of Religion, 63*(1). 124-125.

Stevens, R.A. (2014). Understanding gay identity development within the college environment. *Journal of College Student Development*, *45*, 185-206.

The Bible (2011). New International Version, Biblica.

Tracy, David (1981). *The Analogical Imagination: Christian Theology and the Culture of Pluralism*. Crossroad Publishing.

Tsao, Tiffany (2019). Beyond the binary: A note on translating. In *Sergius Seeks Bacchus* by Norman E. Pasaribu. Tilted Axis Press.

Wehr, Demaris S. (1987). *Jung and Feminism: Liberating Archetypes*. Author Beacon Press.

6
Skin Colour Hierarchy

The Ideal Filipina Beauty and the Conflict of Colour

Cr Patricia Mary Hodge

Introduction: Colonialism and Colourism

Cut.com has a popular YouTube series called "100 Years of Beauty" which traces the beauty standards of various countries across the world in the last century. The video focused on the Philippines features a Filipina with *kayumanggi*[1] skin as the national standard of beauty in the 1910s and 1920s, followed by a light-skinned model from the 1930s onwards into the 2010s. (Cut, 2015). In less than two minutes, the video acknowledges the internalised colourism in a country where the majority of the native population is naturally dark-skinned. The archipelago country of the Philippines is a post-multi-colonial nation with an ethnic and cultural diversity that it owes to its long history of contact with various peoples of the world. The Chinese, with whom the Philippines had trade relations since the 9th century BC brought with them their ideal of the white-powdered beauty and its heavy connotations of class, prestige, status and power, which was later amplified after the occupation of the country by the Spanish, Americans and Japanese. Even during the Spanish rule, the Chinese who had settled in the Philippines received superior treatment that differentiated them from the native population. It was during the Spanish rule that society in the Philippines was divided into a hierarchy of the classes based on economic importance that was in turn determined by genealogy: the Spanish and Spanish *mestizos*, the Chinese, the Chinese *mestizos* and lastly the *indios* or the native population of Malay descent (Wickberg,

1964, p. 63). By the time the Americans came to rule the Philippines, centuries of rule under fair-skinned foreigners had ingrained the belief that to be fair meant higher social standing and economic prosperity. This internalised colourism continues to negatively impact Filipino society, leaving transgenerational psychological scars that cannot be erased.

Ronald Hall (2001, 2006) establishes his research into colourism and race in the Asian community within a global context through a post-colonial lens. He asserts that the power relationships and imbalance in the Asian-Western relationship are endorsed by colonialism and the combined efforts of global and regional conceptualizations of colour and power to determine interracial relationships. In the Asian community, skin colour has attained social and political power, creating differences of class and privilege between the light-skinned Asian community and the dark-skinned Asian community. The privilege associated with being white was exalted by the white coloniser, and then imposed upon the natives who internalised the notion that white is better and beneficial. As Fanon (2008) explains, the once colonised people still "epidermalise" the notion of the superiority of whiteness and the inferiority of blackness, causing friction and tension within racialised groups (p. 80). This intersection of colour, race and social hierarchy in a post-colonial context reveals itself in Filipino socio-economic relationships which are now dominated by the *mestizo*, a social class born out of interactions and intermarriages between local inhabitants and the foreigners who once dominated and colonised them. George Lipsitz (1998) asserts that "whiteness has a cash value", linking the appreciation of whiteness with its privilege to profit from discrimination in the employment market (p. vii). Filipinos with *mestizo* heritage have continued to occupy the highest positions in the political, economic and social life of the country. This colourism is strongly prevalent and heavily visible in the field of beauty. The influence of Western standards of beauty that are remnants of its colonial history, and the influence of globally influential neighbouring East Asian countries have further contributed to the belief that the *tisay*[2] and not the *kayumanggi* is aesthetically pleasing.

The Global Ideal Asian/Filipina Beauty

Gunther Kress and Theo Van Leeuwen (2002) point out that the semiotics of colour occur in two ways, through cultural associations and the past, and from current advertising and branding (p. 355). The globalisation of the market and media has been responsible for the promotion of interregional media which has resulted in the popular culture of East and South-east Asia to attain the status of a global mass culture beyond geographical boundaries. Leo Ching (2001) states "Today, 'Asia' itself is neither a misrepresentation of the Orientalist nor the collective representation of the anti-imperialists. 'Asia' has become a market, and 'Asianness' has become a commute commodity circulating globally through late capitalism." (pp. 305-306). As a result, the fair woman with 'Asian' features such as rounded eyes with double eyelids, a defined nose and jaw, who is fair, slim and tall is the ideal beauty in the dominating countries of East Asia, namely, South Korea, Japan and China. This has been compounded by the pronounced popularity of K-pop, and the consequent consumption of Korean/ Japanese makeup, the popularity of common East Asian skin care, the fetishization of Asian girls and submissive, child-like behaviour like the Korean "aegyo" and Japanese "kawaii", the spread of Japanese Harajiku fashion into Western circles, etc. This has also led to the global fashion and makeup community now focusing on East Asia.

A consequence of the voyeuristic tendency of the Western eye to focus on the Asian's face and body is the assumption of a homogeneous Asia: that the people of Asia all look and behave the same. The fair, tall and thin idol, actress or model gracing television screens and magazines has been successfully established globally as the ideal Asian beauty. This "Asian" beauty follows in the footsteps of the fair, tall and thin Western beauty, and now the native women of these nations whose looks do not comply to these standards have to be further reminded that not only are they inferior because they are not white, they are even more inferior within their own race because they are dark. In a street interview carried out by *AsianBoss* (2018), a female participant identified the features of the ideal Filipina as "a high-bridged nose, whiter skin and slanted eyes." (1:00-1:06). This global and regional fixation upon this "Asian" beauty has worked to cement the position of the fair, tall, Eurasian featured *mestiza* in the Philippines.

King-O'Riain (2006) asserts that "the continued existence of bodies of mixed race does not deconstruct or do away with race" and that the existence of mixed races only adds more layers of signification and nuances to the concept of race (p. 29). The image of the fair, ambiguously featured Asian bears no similarity to the native *moreno* population of the Philippines. The *mestiza*, however is a light skinned Filipina who possesses the mixed heritage and features of the native inhabitant and the fair foreigner. The *mestiza* is therefore, in most cases is a light-skinned Asian or an ambiguous looking, non-threatening to Western sensibilities Eurasian. A mixed-race Filipina with dark skin, however, is undesirable; this obviously being related to the synonymy of dark skin with the inferior native. Skin colour and race are so intrinsically connected that the racial lines along which beauty is conceived in the Philippines remains unquestionable. Colourism in the Philippines thus extends beyond the white-black binary. The mixed-race *mestiza*, instead of alleviating rigid ethnic and racial lines, becomes another racialised being along the lines of beauty.

Responsibility to be Beautiful: Why Fairness Matters

The obsession with beauty is very apparent in the Philippines where beauty pageants are considered a national hobby. The country considers it a matter of pride that the Philippines has been able to produce multiple beauty queens on the international stage. The numerous wins at international pageants by Filipina women, mostly fair skinned *mestizas*, have only furthered the conceptualization of beauty as human capital. Nancy L. Etcoff (1999) points out that the desire to be beautiful is part instinct and part fantasy (p. 43). Beauty is a virtue attached to women, a measure of their social value as well as an indicator of the fantasy of womanly perfection. The responsibility to be beautiful across societies is a task that is placed upon the shoulders of the woman.

Beauty itself is a socially constructed phenomenon, with its own implications of gender, class and race. Appearance, character and abilities are accepted to be complementary factors. This idea stems from colonial assertions of the virtue, dignity and overall superiority of whiteness. While beauty cannot be defined either through science or aesthetic sensibilities, the notion of beauty has been responsible in segregating the 'civilised' from the 'savage', becoming another qualifier in the process of othering. Beauty also determines human behaviour and patterns of acceptance, rejection and admiration because of the assertion of the existence of an inferior that is qualified as ugly. Beauty standards are hurtful to the mental health and self-esteem of women, as they emphasise differences that make one inferior to another, especially when whiteness is a universal standard. In this sense, beauty continues to maintain the racialised hierarchy between people of colour and the white man, and the skin-colour hierarchy among and within the communities of people of colour. Beauty in the Philippines truly lies on the surface: a question of epidermal appearance and melanin, complicated by intersections of race and class. "White is clean, white is pure, white is beautiful" says the actress in an advertisement for a product that promises whiter skin in fourteen days. (CinciRAPP, 2015, 0:00-0:30). Therefore, the process of beautifying oneself with treatments is an activity that has social goals to fulfill, and as such is one that requires financial, physical, emotional and mental investments.

This colourist perception of beauty is furthered by the fact that most female stars in the Philippines and media representations of beautiful women are light skinned *mestizas*. In reference to magazine covers in the Philippines, Encanto (2004) points out that it is the *mestiza* who is the icon of 'femininity', propriety, dress, conduct, class and bearing (p. 19). The beauty industry openly portrays dark skin as something that is negative that must be 'cured'. There are exceptions in the industry. For example, one of the most popular young actresses in the Filipina film industry is Nadine Lustre is a *morena* who is constantly praised by the media for breaking stereotypes. The actress has however admitted to being ashamed of her skin and using bleaching and whitening creams for fear that her acting career would be hampered by her skin colour. While the increasing number of *morena* celebrities embracing their skin colour in a colourist industry is to be applauded, they form a small minority incapable of representing the predominantly *morena* community of the Philippines. On the spectrum of skin colour, these celebrities, especially females, appear to fall in the wheatish to dusky category; thereby still implying that dark is only acceptable when it is a lighter shade of dark. The politics of colourism in the field of beauty has immense consequences owing to the industry's ability to influence social behaviour and expectations. Advertisements and movies encourage the perception the light skin is the norm in a country where the majority of women are not light skinned. Instead this norm is established in everyday life through the means of comparison, thereby making one acutely aware of one's position in the social hierarchy of skin colour.

The popular media and the film industry's stereotypical portrayal of dark skinned Filipinas as maids, or as the laughing stock greatly contribute to the social need to be fair. They are definitively labeled as unattractive while the light skinned Filipina is the ideal beauty. For instance in the popular romantic – *Must be... Love* (Lumibao, D., 2013), the dark skinned native has her love unrequited as the male lead falls for the fair *mestiza*. The lead actress is a *mestiza* herself and had to be tanned in order to play the role of the country-bumpkin, un-lady like Patricia. Robin Tolmach Lakoff and Raquel L. Scherr (1984), state that "the desire for beauty, or at least for attractiveness, possesses every woman, that every woman considers her looks a vital part of herself, that to fail to realize one's full potential for beauty is to feel oneself a failure as a woman and a human being." (p. 12). The inferior dark complexioned Patricia's transformation into the heroine of the movie not only involves her realizing her "full potential for beauty" by lightening her skin by several shades, but also an improvement of her character from ill-mannered tom-boy into a proper lady. The movie embodies the message that being fair is a social capital; it raises a woman's status in society, wins her admiration and gets her the man. The construction of the inferior dark other which has infiltrated the field of beauty coerces the native *morena* to internalise racism and colourism, thereby greatly damaging their self-worth. They become complicit in the process that disadvantages them by reproducing the racism of their erstwhile colonial masters in their own colourist ways in the treatment of their own people.

"Curing" Dark Skin: The Psychological Trauma of Darkness

"Beauty was not just a product of wealth, but a commodity in and of itself. In other words, it was no longer a matter of looking to wealth to find beauty, but of looking to beauty to find status. Now beauty could give the illusion of wealth." (Lakoff and Scherr, 1984, p. 80). Skin colour carries assumptions of one's class, a pre-colonial remnant that fair skin denotes wealth while dark skin would denote that one belonged to the labouring class. The dark skinned *morena* is told that she must strive for her fair skinned *mestiza* counterpart's beauty, and in order to do that she needs to lighten her skin. Explaining the legitimization of cosmetic procedures as part of the female responsibility to be beautiful, Kathy Davis (2002) traces how the field of medicine has historically defined the female body as deficient and in need of repair and so "cosmetic surgery is easily legitimated as a "natural" and, therefore, acceptable therapy for women's problems with their appearance." (p. 55). To come to the *morena* woman's aid, the market in the Philippines is saturated with products that can 'cure' dark skin. Mercury laced creams are banned by the government, yet they still flow into the country and are easily available, despite multiple reports of mercury poisoning among women. Francine Singson (2017) attributes the success of the skin-whitening industry in the Phillipines to the psychological state of the native population due to the American colonial rule, and points to the colonial mentality and the mental health repercussions of the internalization of their oppression. The growing consumption of skin lightening products in the Philippines is a testament to the prevalence of colourism and the hierarchy of social status based on skin shades. The worth of women especially is heavily dependent upon physical appearance, with skin colour being a determining factor of attractiveness.

The result of the skin colour hierarchy is very simple: if one is fair, one is beautiful and can rise in status; if one is ugly, it must be remediated for the sake of upward social mobility. Interestingly, the desire is not to attract the attention of others to the fact that one lightens their skin, as that would make obvious the fact that one is naturally dark-skinned; instead it is to avert attention by blending into the crowd of the 'normal' fair. Consequently, *morena* women attempt to attain the privilege of the light skin *mestizo* through the use of skin-lightening treatments. Advertisements for skin lightening products naturally feature the *mestiza*, because she looks racially ambiguous enough that the female *morena* population accepts her as one of their own, yet she is different enough to be a standard of beauty because of her fair skin. The decision of *morena* women to lighten their skin is thus a pragmatic response to the social and economic situation in the country that privileges the *tisay* over the *kayumaggi.* While this could be viewed as an appropriation of power by mimicking the whiteness of the colonial master and the superior *mestiza*, the process involves the reiteration of the inferiority of the native *morena* in the attempt to appear racially ambiguous through unhealthy and even dangerous methods. Those of lower socio-economic status are more likely to use skin whiteners to try to improve their current situation. According to a study carried out by Mendoza (2014), women of lower socio-economic status were identified frequent and loyal users of skin whitening products. The connection made is that the achievement of the national aesthetic brings along with it improved economic and social status. Skin lightening has become such an accepted part of the Filipina woman's existence that the structure of society, economy and media supports this necessity to be fair skinned. A dark complexion is, thus, a remediable commodity.

The impact upon the mental health and self-esteem of women in the Philippines due to the politics of colour is one that is extremely unhealthy and has not been much studied upon. The *mestiza,* who is the definition of the ideal beauty, is genetically the way she is. The *morena*, in order to become like her has to undergo the time consuming and dangerous process of skin lightening, essentially diminishing her native *morena* identity to look like a mixed-race Filipina. Fanon (2008) points out that the black native, "having been made inferior, proceeds from humiliating insecurity through strongly voiced self-accusation to despair." (p. 43). This leads to a desire on the native's part to essentially reject his body in a process of what Fanon terms to "denaturalize" and "deracialize" himself (p. 52). This desire to "deracialize" in the field of beauty can be understood more clearly in the context of what Margaret Hunter (2007) refers to as the "beauty queue" where ". . . sexism and racism interact to create a queue of women from the lightest to the darkest, where the lightest get the most resources and the darkest get the least. The lightest women get access to more resources because not only are they lighter-skinned and therefore racially privileged, but their light skin is interpreted in our culture as more beautiful and therefore they are also privileged as beautiful women." (pp. 70-71). This ranking in the beauty queue begins explicitly in the intimate circles of family and friends, thus influencing female conception of beauty and its values, which are then acted out and upon in the larger sphere of society. Women are made to feel ashamed of their dark skin as they are continuously bombarded with images across multiple platforms that paint them as undesirable and ugly. This shame of or contempt for their skin is understood better in the light of Horace Romano Harré's (1983) notion of the "body", taking it to mean specifically the skin as a "legible" surface from which the moral judgment can be read" (p. 79) and Fanon's notion of "epidermalization of inferiority" (p. 80). In this context, it can be recognised that the colonial remnant of colourism has continued to pervade and negatively affect the people the colonisers once margianialised, and how it has constructed beauty in the Philippines.

Conclusion

Beauty is of such value that it can negatively affect women with feelings of self-hatred, inferiority complexes and sustain the normalisation of unethical means to achieve self-destructive ideals of beauty. Women in the Philippines are taught on a daily basis by intimate family circles, larger society and the media that they possess an almost moral responsibility to be beautiful. Beauty implies that one is relevant, desired, visible, accepted and included in cultural conversation. The emotional power of exclusion or dismissal as causal factors of mental trauma cannot be underestimated. Beauty, after all for women is more than just appearance; it is heavily associated with feelings of self-confidence and worth. The feeling of contentment is one that women are not allowed to peacefully achieve as they battle both physically and psychologically with generations of socially sanctioned colourism and personal battles of self and group identity. The combined force of skin colour hierarchy in society and the growing market for skin lightening products only sustains that colonial hierarchy of the white superior and the dark native inferior. This striving for whiteness is a common transnational construction that defines the mentality of the individuals living in post-colonial nations. The superiority of whiteness has evolved with the combined influence of colonialism and modern, popular motives which have encouraged the skin-whitening industry. The implicit message nonetheless remains that the fair skinned woman is beautiful, and for this the skin-whitening industry is perceived as needed. This construction and its connotations of beauty do not allow women to heal from the multiple oppressions upon their gender that limits their physical agency and mental health. The relationship between colourism, economic neo-imperialism and the economic and social considerations of beauty has an intricate relationship of co-dependency resulting in societal expectations and tendencies that are heavily colourist and gendered. It is necessary first to challenge the structural colourist hierarchy of the *mestiza-morena* and matters of representation in order for there to be any resolution regarding the beauty standards of the Philippines. The question thus remains as to how the women in the Phillipines are to heal from the numerous conflicts within them and with society as they are forced to partake in this inherited struggle to be beautiful.

NOTES

1. The Tagalog word for brown. The word is closely associated with dusky, tan or "brown" complexion. It is also an alternative word for, or is synonymous with *moreno*. As a concept and a sign, *kayumanggi* carries semiotic connotations of race, class and gender.
2. *Tisay* is an alternative word for *mestizo*, and is understood to indicate white-skin or fair-skin. It is more commonly used to indicate the female gender, as is *kayumanggi*.

REFERENCES

AsianBoss. (2018, Oct. 26). *What's The Ideal Beauty Standard In The Philippines?* [Video]. YouTube. https://youtu.be/3QDB7mqCjRI

CinciRAPP. (2015, Aug. 19). *Skin Whitening Commercials* [Video]. YouTube. https://www.youtu.be/3QDB7mqCjRI

Ching, Leo. (2001). Globalizing the Regional, Regionalizing the Global: Mass Culture and Asianism in the Age of Late Capital. In Arjun Appadurai (Ed), *Globalization* (pp. 279-306), Duke University Press. https://doi.org/10.1215/9780822383215-017

Cut. (2015, May 19). *Philippines (April)|100 Years of Beauty - Ep 6* [Video]. YouTube. https://www.youtu.be/NIsAeFYZFXE

Davis, Kathy. (2002). A Dubious Equality: Men, Women and Cosmetic Surgery. *Body & Society, 8*(1), pp. 49-65.

Encanto, Georgina Reyes. (2002). *Constructing the Filipina: A History of Women's Magazines 1891-2002*. University of the Philippines Press.

Etcoff, Nancy L. (1999). *Survival of the Prettiest: The Science of Beauty*. Doubleday.

Fanon, Frantz. (2008). *Black Skin, White Masks*. Translated by Charles Lam Markmann, Pluto Press. (Original work published 1952).

Hall, Ronald. (2001). *Filipina Eurogamy: Skin Color as a Vehicle of Psychological Colonization*. Giraffe Books.

Hall, Ronald. (2006). *Beaching Beauty: Light Skin as a Filipina Ideal*. Giraffe Books.

Harré, Horace R. (1983). *Physical Being*. Blackwell.

Hunter, Margaret. (2007). *Race, Gender, and the Politics of Skin Tone*. Routledge.

King-O'Riain and Rebecca Chiyoko. (2006). *Pure Beauty: Judging Race in Japanese American Beauty Pageants*. University of Minnesota Press.

Kress, G. and T. van Leeuwen. (2002). Colour as a Semiotic Mode: Notes for a Grammar of Colour. *Visual Communication, 1*(3), pp. 343-368.

Lakoff, Robin and Raquel, L. Scherr (1984). *Face Value: The Politics of Beauty.* Routledge.

Lipsitz, George (1998). *The Possessive Investment in Whiteness: How White People Profit from Identity Politics*. Temple University Press.

Lumibao, D. (Director). (2013). *Must be ... Love.* Star Cinema.

Mendoza, R.L. (2014). The Skin Whitening Industry in the Philippines. *Journal of Public Health Policy, 35*(2), 219-238. https://doi:org/10.1057/jphp.2013.50.

Singson, F. (2017). Colonialism's Røle in the Success of the Filipino Skin Whitening Industry. *Auctus: The Journal of Undergraduate Research and Creative Scholarship,* pp. 1-11.

Wickberg, E. (1964). The Chinese Mestizo in Philippine History. *The Journal of South-east Eastern History, 5*(1), 62-100. https://doi.org/10.1017/S0217781100002222

Section III

7

A Study of the Relationship between Environmental Change, Migration and Conflict

The South-South-east Asian Scenario

Bennathaniel H. Diengdoh, Batriti Nongbri and *Tiewri Lyngdoh-Nonglait*

Introduction

Environmental change, in the form of climate change, sea level rise, resource depletion and their implications cannot be ignored. Four routes for changes in the concentration of atmospheric greenhouse gases (GHGs) have been put forth by Moss *et al.* (2008), which trace out the projected increases in the quantities of GHGs over the course of the 21st century. These Representative Concentration Pathways (RCPs): RCP 2.6, RCP 4.5, RCP 6.0 and RCP 8.5 (Moss *et al.*, 2008) predict global mean surface temperature increases with mean upper limits of 3.7°C (IPCC, 2014) by the year 2100. Predictions have been made of sea level rise (SLR) due to thermal expansion of oceans with upper limits of almost 40cm above mean sea level (Gregory, 2013). Other researchers have also found evidence of gradual SLR, though their findings show variation as to the extent (Church & White, 2006; Ablain *et al.*, 2009[1]).

Increases in sea level would put low-lying coastal regions at high risk of inundation, which would lead to the considerable displacement of individuals and give rise to mass movements of refugees, displaced persons and migrants. Resource depletion due to overexploitation could possibly lead to conflict between different interest groups. If populations increase due to migration, pressure mounting on valuable resources such as water, wood, land and food supply and issues over access and usage rights may increase the probability of conflict (Reuveny, 2007).

Population growth, resource intensive living standards and increasingly mobile populations, may increase tensions that could lead to conflict as environmental problems exacerbate. Conflicts may arise not only between different populations (e.g. hosts and immigrants; see Reuveny, 2007) but also within a population or group, at times over important but dwindling resources (Pomeroy, *et al.*, 2007).

A number of countries comprising South-South-east Asia boast extensive coastlines and low-lying areas, which are vulnerable to the impacts of climate change and sea level rise. Mass migration induced by environmental issues is likely to present countries in the region with a host of dilemmas, ranging from changes in the political arena (such as whether or not to accept such populations) to logistical challenges (such as the allocation adequate areas, supplies and amenities to immigrant populations). Tensions and conflicts between immigrant and host populations may arise at varying scales along ethnic, socio-cultural and/or religious lines over resources such as land, accommodation, employment, water.

The objective of this chapter is to re-examine the relationship between environmental issues such as resource depletion, climate change, sea level rise, environmental impact induced migration, and conflict and to elucidate the additional influencing factors, with focus on a possible future scenario for the South-South-east Asia region.

Environmental Change, Dwindling Resources and Their Relationship with Conflict

Environmental change in the form of climate change or resource depletion, may serve to catalyse conflict between different social groups. As Theisen *et al.* (2013) argue, if precipitation levels decline as temperatures rise, the instances of poverty will correspondingly increase in scale, as would the chances of conflict occurring as the ability to acquire and utilize natural resources decreases. Agriculture, animal husbandry and associated productivity would be affected. The scarcity of rainfall and consequent economic impacts caused affected people of lower socio-economic strata in Brazil to intrude upon larger plots of land, especially in areas where the land distribution is considered to be unequal (Hidalgo *et al.*, 2010). Conflict is far more likely to arise along pre-existing "fault-lines" (Reuveny, 2007, p. 659) such as socio-economic divides, as well as other differences such as ethno-linguistic, cultural and religious ones within a population itself, either pre-existing or which may have been brought about by the migration.

Natural resources such as water, soil and vegetation enable populations to survive, facilitate productivity and enable the acquisition of wealth and income. Although some resources may be viewed as 'renewable', they may in fact, be limited (Ayling and Kelly, 1997, p.182); they could be vulnerable to pollution, degradation or require time to regenerate once exploited. Access to them may be restricted by property rights and access regimes, which, if lacking in clarity could make the issue more complex (Ayling and Kelly, 1997). Conflict over resources may arise between interest groups such as immigrants and natives if usage rights and regimes are ambiguous and resources are rare (Reuveny, 2007).

The political landscape of a nation or a region has an important role to play in influencing the cause-effect relationships that characterise environmental conflict and mitigation. At first, the general consensus was that such conflicts arose as a result of poverty or decline in available resources and the dynamics of supply and demand (Homer-Dixon, 2010). In other words, as resources decline and/or become rarer, interest groups will compete for them with increasing rigor, and conflict would manifest with greater frequency and intensity. However, conflicts arising from or in relation to environmental issues are nuanced and subject to the interplay of a wide variety of factors including political, socio-cultural, economic, religious aspects (Reuveny, 2007).

Climate change, sea level rise and resource depletion are issues not only of environmental importance but of political significance as well, as efforts to address them are matters of national policy, and international cooperation, among others. For example, migration that may be caused by SLR induced inundation of low-lying areas especially across international borders, would inevitably bring immigrants and refugees into contact with host populations. Where such contact occurs, the possibility of conflict arising for any number or variety of reasons is ever present.

Conflicts described as environmental in nature are subject to the influence of a wide variety of factors such as climate, and the quality of air and water, the availability of natural resources and their exploitation etc. In the past, examples of such conflicts have been elucidated with the intention of illuminating the cause-effect relationship between environmental issues and conflict (Libiszewski, 1991; Ayling and Kelly, 1997). However, as we shall discuss below, not all environmental issues inevitably lead to conflict. Natural resource depletion (e.g. loss of forest cover, loss of ground water etc.) has environmental and social implications for communities that depend on them. Disputes could arise over access and usage rights. If the dispute is between two nations or states, this lends a political dimension to the issue.

Collier and Hoeffler (1998) found that the availability of natural resources increases the likelihood of civil war, and can prolong its duration in the beginning, but eventually leads to a decrease in both. Turner (2004) opines that environmental conflicts that take place in a region can be examined from the point of view of environmental security, (i.e. the dangers posed by environmental problems) and from that of the administration of what is regarded as common property. These perspectives seek to explore and elucidate how declining resource pools and corresponding availability can lead to conflict. However, scholars have contributed to framing more intricate and multifaceted views of such conflicts (Turner, 2004). Issues that affect environmental security can have adverse effects on employment, security and the socio-economic and political milieu of a region as well (Hassan *et al.*, 2017).

Environmental issues can cause conflict, but the nature and distribution of conflicts differ with location, scale and the populations involved. Environmental problems and corresponding conflicts vary in scale and affect different geographical regions, socio-economic strata, ethnic and cultural groups differently. Conflicts may even exist at smaller scales such as those arising over the extraction of sand in India (Martínez-Alier, 2018).

Conflicts over resources may be given further nuance if at least one of the interest groups involved are an immigrant population seeking refuge in another nation, or geographical territory of their own country. This however, is founded upon the possibility that environmental change leads to migration, which is discussed below.

Does Environmental Change lead to Migration?

Lee's Push and Pull Theory (1966) dwelt upon the various factors and issues that influence human migration. Factors that render an environment less suitable for habitation, and cause residents to consider migrating elsewhere are dubbed push factors. Pull factors are those that are viewed as improving habitability and living standards, in turn attracting potential migrants.

For example, political turmoil, martial conflict and war may serve to act as push factors causing populations to migrate away from conflict zones. Impressions of a peaceful, conflict free, higher standard of living elsewhere, may be considered as pull factors that attract such migrants and refugees. Conflict in Syria, which began in 2010, had led to the migration of nearly 2 million refugees to neighbouring Turkey by 2015 seeking to escape from the war (Bahcekapili & Cetin, 2015). Push and pull factors encompass a wide variety of economic, political, cultural and environmental issues that play a role in determining the nature and direction of migration including environmental push factors such as earthquakes, volcanic eruptions, cyclones, sea level rise and socio-economic pull factors such as better employment opportunities, improved living standards among others (Diengdoh & Lyngdoh, 2016).

When faced with environmental disasters and/or political upheaval, populations may attempt to migrate to destination regions that they consider to be safer, more abundant in resources, provisions, and thus more suitable for habitation. Populations will choose migration if the "net benefit (total benefit minus total cost) from migrating is larger than that from not migrating" (Reuveny, 2007:658). In Nepal, increases in population and land use change resulted in a decline in available resources for residents causing out migration over short and great distances with impacts that varied across different age groups, gender and ethnicity (Massey *et al.*, 2010).

Migration is not always a feasible option for populations faced with environmental disaster or socio-political unrest. As Tacoli (2009) opines, migration requires means, chiefly financial resources, and the ability of existing social structures to support and facilitate it. Both of these, according to her (Tacoli, 2009), may only decline in terms of availability as climate change progresses.

Moreover, as Van Hear (2006) states, in light of increasingly strict regulations placed on international migration, mobility depends upon financial means, social capital and probability, the first two of which, he describes as being influenced greatly by the socio-economic status of migrants.

Once They Arrive: Migrant-Host Dynamics

Once migration has begun, several challenges arise. Firstly, its immigration policy will determine if and how immigrants will be accepted. Immigrants may be prevented from joining the native populace or they may be allowed to enter on a temporary basis, restrictions of which may or may not be rigorously enforced (Huguet & Punpuing, 2005). Secondly, resources must be allotted and diverted to meet the needs of immigrants, and more so if said immigrants become long term or permanent residents. For example, immigrants can eventually compete with natives for employment opportunities (Bahcekapili & Cetin, 2015). Government agencies have to navigate the issue of providing for the needs of both groups while avoiding to the best possible ability, arousing resentment in either, particularly, in host populations. If resources are inadequate, increasing populations due to migration could put more pressure on them, giving rise to competition, and possibly, conflict (Reuveny, 2007). Thirdly, if migrants seek and are granted asylum, protracted contact with host populations is inevitable, which could lead to conflict. Should conflict arise, it falls upon government agencies to resolve it and restore peace and order.

Reuveny (2007) argues that while developed countries (DCs) are highly likely to address the needs and implications that arise with the influx of such populations innovatively through advances in technology and "institutional redesign" (p. 657), it is less likely that developing countries will be able to do the same successfully, due to a paucity of resources and knowledge.

Thus, manifestation and exacerbation of tensions between host and immigrant populations depend on factors such as availability of resources, government policy with regards to amenities and benefits given to the latter, among others. As immigrant populations amass, the likelihood of said immigrants violating the laws and customs of the host population will probably increase, which would likely instigate new tensions or worsen existing ones.

Is Conflict Inevitable?

We have established that a relationship exists between environmental issues such as resource depletion, climate change, sea level rise etc. migration and conflict. Competition for valuable resources as well as various socio-cultural divides between host and immigrant populations can lead to conflict. However, the subsequent question that arises is whether or not conflict is an inevitable outcome of host-immigrant interactions.

Reuveny (2007) highlights 38 instances of migration, only half of which led to conflict. For example, migration from El Salvador to Honduras and eventually to the United States in the late 1960s, which occurred due to a combination of environmental and socio-economic factors, led to violent conflict, most notably, the 100 Hours War of 1969 (Durham, 1992; Myers, 1993; Reuveny, 2007; Homer-Dixon, 2010; see also Wilson, 2008; Martz, 1978 and Anderson, 1981). Boyden *et al.* (2002) recount how harsh government responses to occasionally aggressive protests by minorities in Bhutan led to considerable numbers leaving for Nepal, while the rights of those who remained behind were curtailed.

Reuveny (2007) also reviews other instances such as that of migration in Ecuador, due to several reasons (including environmental issues), that caused no notable conflict (Pichon & Bilsborrow, 1999; Bilsborrow, 2002; Reuveny, 2007). Nordås & Gleditsch (2007) posit that those fleeing environmental change or disasters do not, or would not have the same motives, plans or agendas as populations moving or migrating for socio-political reasons. They imply that it is highly improbable that such migrants would either seek or be equipped to actively cause conflict.

Ware (2005) discusses the significance of the interplay of population, demographics and available land resources in Pacific island nations. Ware (2005) states that on some islands, the population is concentrated in small areas, which could catalyse conflict, while on others, the population is so small, that even basic amenities cannot be maintained. Such a lack would encourage individuals to emigrate to more populated islands, which could further depopulate the already sparsely inhabited islands and lead to overpopulation at densely inhabited ones.

It is evident that conflict is not an inescapable result of environmental issues such as resource depletion or climate change/ SLR induced migration. Whether or not conflict occurs is subject to case by case nuances that may exist between host and immigrant populations. These factors, either acting independently or (and most commonly) acting in tandem can facilitate conflict.

The South-South-east Asian Scenario:Conflict Facilitating Factors

South-South-east Asia is a region of ethnic, cultural, geographical and biological diversity. However, there are populations in the region vulnerable to environmental problems such as climate change and sea level rise. In light of possible future impacts of such problems, mass movements of people may intensify over the course of the 21st century. We have elucidated that conflict is not a necessary outcome of migration, and is subject to a number of facilitating factors. We discuss at length, in the section below, the factors that could instigate or catalyse conflict in the region in the future.

1. The Political Milieu: Underlying Differences of Opinion

Migration, particularly across geopolitical divides, notably in the form of mass movements across international borders can lead to dramatic changes in the ethnic, racial and demographic profile of the host nation or region. Illegal migration can become a source of tension between nations as the host countries labour to address the varied issues arising from influx. It may also foster a lack of trust between them, as each nation may view the other with suspicion (Reuveny, 2007).

Boyden *et al.* (2002) list a considerable number of governance related factors that instigate conflict throughout South Asia, including, *inter alia*, "lack of ethos in public service", "rigged elections", and a dearth of political accountability of governments in issues related to human rights and conflict (pp. 16-33).

Illegal migrants may end up playing a role in vote bank politics, as political leaders may take the opportunity to exploit said populations' insecurity by providing shelter, basic amenities and employment in exchange for political support. Conflicts that arise due to other factors will invariably be undergirded by the political milieu of each respective region.

Migration across borders in Asia has in the past, only been viewed as acceptable on a non-permanent basis due to the fact most are relatively young nations emerging from decades of foreign colonization, and also because of a perceived desire by natives to maintain a homogenous culture (Hugo, 2005). Pro-immigration policies may not sit well with a host population that values homogeneity, and/or is faced with issues of resource scarcity, competition for employment, and an aging or minority population.

Differences of opinion with regards to land tenure, access to resources or employment between host and immigrant populations will likely make their way into political arena. The naturalization of immigrant populations could bestow upon them rights and franchise by which they may be able to influence the political landscape of the host region. Gradual changes may foster resentment in host populations who may come to view immigrants as unwelcome elements bringing about undesired change in the socio-economic, political, ethnic and demographic profile of the region. For example, based upon his study of the state of Nagaland, Singh (2009) concluded that the presence of illegal immigrants in North-Eastern India could give rise to and exacerbate tensions between the immigrants and natives, and bring about a change in the demographics and the political profile of the entire region. Pre-existing tensions, political turmoil or conflicts at the destination or host region could also raise the risk of conflict (Reuveny, 2007). Boyden *et al.* (2002) highlight that conflicts in South Asia have a long intricate history, making mitigation and resolution very difficult.

2. Ethnic, Religious and Cultural Divides

South-South-east Asia is populated by a great variety of races, tribes and ethnic groups, hailing from regions of varied geography, topography, biological, religious and cultural diversity. Since religion and culture are often interwoven, religious differences often express themselves as cultural differences as well. Mass movements of people within the bounds of the Indian sub-continent have already brought about tensions between populations, many such incidents being between host and migrant ethnic groups. For example, tense relations exist between native Bengali, and North-east Indian populations and those who have migrated from Bangladesh (e.g. Swain, 1996; Reuveny, 2007; Homer-Dixon, 2010). Sukma (2005) cites ethnic divides as causes for conflict in Kalimantan, Indonesia and also elucidates the fact that some arose between different ethnic groups belonging to the same religion.

We posit that religious and cultural differences can represent another of what Reuveny (2007: 659) calls "fault-lines" along which conflict may occur. Hugo (2005) describes Asians' desire to maintain the integrity of their culture as one of the reasons some countries have resisted giving permanent residence to migrants in the past. If immigrants are from a different culture and ethnic group, and/or subscribe to a different belief system than that of the natives, religious and/or cultural tension may arise. Clashes between Indian host and Bangladeshi migrant populations in West Bengal and the North-east have typically begun along religious divides (Swain, 1996; Homer-Dixon, 2010). Sukma (2005) cites religious differences as strong instigating factors in the conflicts between host Christian populations and migrants from Bugis, Buton and Makassar in Indonesia. It must be noted that cultural and non-cultural conflicts in South-east Asia have been taking place at comparable frequencies from 1945-2007(Croissant &Trinn, 2009). Various conflicts start along lines of ethnicity but turn into interreligious conflicts like those in Ambon, Maluku (Sukma, 2005). Attacks against religious minorities often lead to various atrocities, involving the looting of properties and places of worship; 4071 such attacks were reported in Bangladesh from 2007-2018 (Odhikar, 2019).

3. Land Use, Resource Access and Employment

Land use, access to resources, usufruct rights and competition for employment can also become points of contention between immigrants and natives. If immigrant populations increase, a combination of rising demand, rare or depleting resources and ambiguous regulations among other factors could catalyse competition between populations and raise the possibility of conflict (Reuveny, 2007). In areas owned and administered by local communities, traditional institutions and forms of government, pressure brought about by a massive influx of immigrants may compel local institutions to provide aid, supplies, and accommodation. If these are inadequate, immigrant populations may exploit the option acquiring them from property owned and administered by local people with or without official permission. Even if permission is granted, it would likely be conditional. If immigrants violate the conditions, tension and conflict could arise. Ambiguous property rights and resource access regimes over dwindling resources could also spark conflict within a population as well (Pomeroy *et al.*, 2007). The Thai Government, while acquiring natural resources in the border areas of northern Thailand chose not to include all minorities into its integration programme for fear of exacerbating internal migration issues (Vaddhanaphuti, 2005). Conflicts between minorities and the government over occupancy of forested areas became common during the 1990s (Vaddhanaphuti, 2005). In Cambodia, conflicts in inland fisheries were mainly caused by ineffective administration and inadequate policy enactment (Salayo *et al.*, 2006). Conflicts over fisheries in the Visayan Sea in the Philippines were exacerbated by policies restricting access of fishing fleets to specified fishing areas (Salayo *et al.*, 2006).

Immigrants may, if given the opportunity, seek employment opportunities to support themselves. In Thailand, it has been opined that immigrants may be willing to work for longer hours and less remuneration (Martin, 2007). If faced with a choice, employers are likely to hire a workforce that will bring them maximum profits at minimal cost. If immigrants prove to be less demanding as employees than natives, the likelihood of the former being hired instead of the latter will increase. Immigrants become competition for local populations for employment (Reuveny, 2007; Singh, 2009; Bahcekapili & Cetin, 2015) particularly in the informal sector, at times, taking up jobs that hosts desire (Bahcekapili & Cetin, 2015). In Malaysia, Hugo (2005) states that the majority of illegal immigrants were involved in what he described as the "3D (dirty, dangerous and difficult)" jobs (p. 24). Depending upon cultural and social perceptions, these jobs may not be preferred by the local populace. If, however, natives are interested in them, competition and conflict may arise. Migrant workers in Thailand also took up occupations viewed as less preferable to natives (Martin, 2007). In the same country, immigrants displaced from Myanmar though prohibited from leaving their confinement areas but would do so in search of work (Huguet & Punpuing, 2005). Those who entered Thailand seeking employment would do so on short-term passes that would elapse but were however eventually regularized and given permits to be employed while remaining classified as illegal (Huguet & Punpuing, 2005).

Accessibility and availability of resources often shares a direct relationship with socio-economic status. Even among migrants, greater financial wealth is likely to not only facilitate and expedite migration, but also afford potential migrants the privilege of choosing where to migrate (Van Hear, 2006), and (if permissible) gain access to resources, facilities, amenities and capital at their selected destination.

Financial resources play a greater role than other forms of capital in the determination of the mobility of an individual or a population (Van Hear, 2006). If immigrants lack financial capital, they are far more likely to become dependent upon state provided benefits and amenities. This may cause tension between them and host populations, especially if resources are scarce.

Conclusion

Conflict within a population or between immigrant and host populations caused by environmental change induced migration and/or due to global warming, sea level rise and/or dwindling resources is a notable possibility. In the South-South-east Asia region, conflicts have arisen in the past within communities over depleting resources, but notably, most have mainly arisen along ethnic and religious lines. As environmental change in the form of depleting resources, global warming, sea level rise and climate change continues to manifest, internal as well as inter-state migration is likely to continue, which may in turn instigate future conflict. The purpose of this chapter is to highlight the possibility and influencing factors of conflict in the region with the view of aiding in preventive and preparatory policy making to mitigate such issues in the future.

Acknowledgement: We wish to express our gratitude towards Mr. B.B. Wahlang, Dr. B. Shabong and Dr. R.B. Kharkongor for their invaluable input during the writing of this chapter.

NOTE

1. See: Nicholls, R.J., and A. Cazenave. Sea-level Rise and its Impact on Coastal Zones. *Science, 328*(5985) (2010): 1517-1520.

REFERENCES

Ablain, M., Cazenave, A., Valladeau, G., & Guinehut, S. (2009). A new assessment of the error budget of global mean sea level rate estimated by satellite altimetry over 1993-2008. *Ocean Science*, *5*(2), 193-201. https://doi.org/https://doi.org/10.5194/os-5-193-2009

Anderson, T.P. (1981). *The war of the dispossessed: Honduras and El Salvador,* 1969. University of Nebraska PR.

Ayling, R., and Kelly, K. (1997). Dealing with conflict: Natural resources and dispute resolution. The Commonwealth Forestry Review, *76*(3), 182-185.

Retrieved February 19, 2021, from http://www.jstor.org/stable/42608590

Bahcekapili, C., & Cetin, B. (2015). The Impacts of Forced Migration on Regional Economies: The Case of Syrian Refugees in Turkey. *International Business Research, 8*(9). https://doi.org/10.5539/ibr.v8n9p1

Bilsborrow, R.E. (2002). Migration, population change, and the rural environment. *Environmental Change and Security Project Report, 8*(1), 69-84.

Boyden, J., de Berry, J., Feeny, T., & Hart, J. (2002). *Oxford: Refugee Studies Centre. Children affected by armed conflict in South Asia: A review of trends and issues identified through secondary research.*

Church, J.A., & White, N.J. (2006). A 20th century acceleration in global sea-level rise. *Geophysical Research Letters, 33*(1).

Collier, P., & Hoeffler, A. (1998). On economic causes of civil war. *Oxford Economic Papers, 50*(4), pp. 563-573.

Croissant, A., & Trinn, C. (2009). Culture, identity and conflict in Asia and South-east Asia. *Asien, 110*(S), pp. 13-43.

Diengdoh, B.H., & Lyngdoh, L.M. (2016). In K. Nongrum & A.P. Warjri (Eds.) *Human Migration in South Asia: Dynamics and Implications,* pp. 225-248. Essay, Akansha Publishing House.

Durham, W.H. (1992). *Scarcity and survival in Central America: Ecological Origins of the Soccer War.* Stanford University Press.

Gregory, J. (2013). Projections of sea level rise. *Climate Change.*

Hassan, M., Afridi, M.K., & Khan, M.I. (2017). Environmental diplomacy in South Asia: considering the environmental security, conflict and development nexus. *Geoforum, 82*, pp. 127-130.

Hidalgo, F.D., Naidu, S., Nichter, S., & Richardson, N. (2010). Economic determinants of land invasions. *The Review of Economics and Statistics, 92*(3), pp. 505-523.

Homer-Dixon, T.F. (2010). *Environment, Scarcity, and Violence.* Princeton University Press.

Hugo, G. (2005). *Migration in the Asia-Pacific Region.* Ginebra: Global Commission on International Migration.

Huguet, J.W., & Punpuing, S. (2005). *International Migration in Thailand.* International Organization for Migration, Regional Office Bangkok, Thailand.

IPCC, 2014. *Climate Change 2014: Synthesis Report.* Contribution of Working Groups I, II and III to the Fifth Assessment Report of the Intergovernmental Panel on Climate Change [Core Writing Team, R.K. Pachauri and L.A. Meyer (eds.), IPCC, Geneva, Switzerland.

Lee, E.S. (1966). A Theory of Migration. *Demography, 3*(1), pp. 47-57.

Libiszewski, S. (1991). What is an environmental conflict? *Journal of Peace Research, 28*(4), pp. 407-422.

Martin, P. (2007). *The economic contribution of migrant workers to Thailand: Towards policy development*. Bangkok: ILO.

Martínez-Alier, J. (2018). Ecological distribution conflicts and the vocabulary of environmental justice. In *Ecology, Economy and Society*, pp. 187-204. Springer, Singapore.

Martz, M.J.R. (1978). *The Central American Soccer War: Historical patterns and internal dynamics of OAS settlement procedures,* No. 4. Ohio University, Center for International Studies.

Massey, D.S., Axinn, W.G., & Ghimire, D.J. (2010). Environmental change and out-migration: Evidence from Nepal. *Population and Environment*, *32*(2-3), pp. 109-136.

Moss, R.H., *et al*. (2008). *Towards New Scenarios for Analysis of Emissions, Climate Change, Impacts, and Response Strategies*.

Myers, N. (1993). *Ultimate Security: The Environmental Basis of Political Stability*. WW Norton & Company, Inc.

Nicholls, R.J., & Cazenave, A. (2010). Sea-Level Rise and Its Impact on Coastal Zones. *Science*, *328*(5985), pp. 1517-1520.

Nordås, R., & Gleditsch, N.P. (2007). Climate Change and Conflict. In *Competition and Conflicts on Resource Use,* pp. 21-38. Springer, Cham.

Odhikar. (2019). *Three-month Human Rights Monitoring Report on Bangladesh. Reporting Period: January-March 2019*. Odhikar, 17 April, 2019. http://odhikar.org/wpcontent/uploads/2019/04/HRR_Jannuary-March_2019_Eng.pdf

Pichon, F., & Bilsborrow, R.E. (1999). Land use systems, deforestation, and demographic factors in the humid tropics: farm-level evidence from Ecuador. In R.E. Bilsborrow & D.J. Hogan (Eds.), *Population and Deforestation in the Humid Tropics*, pp. 175-207. Essay, International Union for the Scientific Study of Population.

Pomeroy, R., Parks, J., Pollnac, R., Campson, T., Genio, E., Marlessy, C., & Hue, N.T. (2007). Fish wars: Conflict and collaboration in fisheries management in South-east Asia. *Marine Policy*, *31*(6), pp. 645-656.

Reuveny, R. (2007). Climate change-induced migration and violent conflict. *Political Geography*, *26*(6), pp. 656-673.

Salayo, N., Viswanathan, K., Ahmed, M., & Garces, L. (2006). *An Overview of Fisheries Conflicts in South and South-east Asia: Recommendations, Challenges and Directions*.

Singh, M.A. (2009). *A Study on Illegal Immigration into North-East India: The Case of Nagaland*. Institute for Defence Studies and Analyses, New Delhi, (8), pp. 1-57.

Sukma, R. (2005). Ethnic conflicts in Indonesia: causes and the quest for solution. In *Ethnic Conflicts in South-east Asia*, pp. 1-4.

Swain, A. (1996). Environmental migration and conflict dynamics: focus on developing regions. *Third World Quarterly, 17*(5), pp. 959-974.

Tacoli, C. (2009). Crisis or adaptation? Migration and climate change in a context of high mobility. *Environment and Urbanization, 21*(2), pp. 513-525.

Theisen, O.M., Gleditsch, N.P., & Buhaug, H. (2013). Is climate change a driver of armed conflict?. *Climatic Change, 117*(3), pp. 613-625.

Turner, M. D. (2004). Political ecology and the moral dimensions of "resource conflicts": the case of farmer-herder conflicts in the Sahel. *Political Geography, 23*(7), pp. 863-889.

Vaddhanaphuti, C. (2005). The Thai state and ethnic minorities: From assimilation to selective integration. *Ethnic Conflicts in Southeast Asia*, pp. 151-166.

van Hear, N. (2006). *'I went as far as my money would take me': conflict, forced migration and class*. Forced migration and global processes: A view from forced migration studies, pp. 125-158.

Ware, H. (2005). Demography, migration and conflict in the Pacific. *Journal of Peace Research, 42*(4), pp. 435-454.

Wilson, R. (2008). *The Soccer War : The social implications of a 100 hour war between El Salvador and Honduras.*

8

Impact of Ethnic Conflict on Agriculture and Sustainable Rural Development in Bodoland Territorial Area District (BTAD) in Assam

Kaveri Khound

Introduction

The word "ethnic" has roots to the Greek word "ethnikos" which means race or large groups of people having common traits and customs or groups "in an exotic primitive culture". But the term ethnic or ethnicity entered the lexicon of social science studies only in 1953. An Ethnic Group in general refers to groups of people both small as well as large communities having common traits, customs, culture and aboriginal of a land. The aspiration and cultural dominance of one ethnic group has led to attempts to carve out an exclusive territorial and political space based on being indigenous to the land. This results in the exclusion of the communities that may be labelled as the 'other' or 'outsider' even if they have been historically part of the same territorial and political space. This has invariably resulted in creating strife in the society. Racial and ethnic conflicts among ethnic groups in the present era have become a global feature. Conflicts are deeply rooted in the rapid socio-economic changes taking place in the society and the unequal access to available resources. Diverse ethnic groups sharing a similar resource base are unequally placed in terms of their control of the resource base, particularly land. This unequal power relationship existing among the several ethnic groups, when not controlled, results in conflicts that take the shape of an ethnic conflict.

Assam being a multi-ethnic, multi-lingual, multi-cultural region has always been subjected to various types of ethnic conflicts. The large presence of Bengalis, together with their relatively easy socialization into the native language, has culturally threatened the Assamese and made them insecure in the face of continuous Bengali immigration across the international border with Bangladesh. The larger tribal groups, the Bodos in particular, have similarly felt culturally, economically and politically marginalized. Due to a perceived fear of loss of their land, culture and identity, they have often engaged in violence against other groups especially Muslims and Adivasis that have settled in the Bodoland Territorial Area District. Major ethnic conflicts took place between the Bodos and Muslims as well as the Bodos and Adivasis in the years 1993, 1994, 1996, 1998, 2012 and 2014.

Reoccurring ethnic conflicts in Bodoland have profoundly affected agricultural development in the area. Most of the people are engaged in agricultural work and the land is sown more than once in a year with HYV seeds thus, contributing a large amount to the GDP of Assam. But, repeated conflicts have led to the temporary displacement of people from their villages for months. This has resulted in the reduction of agricultural production as well as leading to changes in the occupation of many of the victimized villagers.

In this chapter an attempt has been made to study the impact of conflict particularly the 2012 ethnic conflict on the agricultural production of Kokrajhar which is the district capital of BTAD using both secondary as well as primary data collected from two villages in Kokrajhar District. The secondary data is collected from research articles, books and newspapers. This data is used to study various ethnic conflicts in Assam especially in Bodoland and to ascertain the impact of ethnic conflicts on the livelihood activities and agriculture of the area. The primary data was collected from two villages of the Gossaigaon Circle in Kokrajhar district. Gossaigaon circle was selected for collecting data since it was the worst affected region during 2012 conflict. During this particular conflict, two ethnic communities were involved, i.e., the Bodos and the Muslims. It was due to this reason that the information on the impact of conflict was collected from Babubil village where the majority of the residents were Muslims and from Boro Binyakhata village where the residents were from the Bodo community. The information was collected through a direct interview method with the help of a questionnaire from 100 households of the two villages. 50 households each from the two villages were surveyed. The questionnaire used in the survey was a mixture of both open ended and close ended questions relating to the 2012 ethnic conflict in Kokrajhar. From the information collected through secondary and primary data, the study presents its analysis and conclusions.

Background of Ethnic Conflict in BTAD

Assam was among the first of the regions to demonstrate signs of severe political crisis on the attainment of India's Independence. Bodos, the largest plains tribes in Assam, initiated an insurgency movement since 1987 demanding for a separate Bodo homeland called 'Bodoland' on the plank of meeting their economic, social and cultural aspirations of the Bodo community. Bodoland Territorial Area District (BTAD) is the ancestral land of the Bodo tribe. The BTAD region in Assam, also known as Bodoland, is the gateway to the North-Eastern India. Bodoland is located in the extreme west of Assam on the northern bank of the Brahmaputra River in the state of Assam in North-East India. The region has both national and international boundaries with the countries of Bhutan and Bangladesh. Bodoland was created very recently in 2003 under the Bodoland Territorial Council Accord by carving out an area of eight districts of Assam namely, Kokrajhar, Dhubri, Bongaigaon, Barpeta, Nalbari, Kamrup, Darrang and Sonitpur within the state of Assam. It is an autonomous administrative unit constituted under the Sixth Schedule of the Constitution of India covering an area of 8,795 sq. km (2011 Census Report). Bodoland is administered by the Bodoland Territorial Council (BTC). BTAD consist of four districts namely Kokrajhar, Udalguri, Chirang and Baksha. At present, Kokrajhar serves as the capital of Bodoland Territorial Area District (BTAD). Bodoland is the home of the "Bodos", an ethnic and linguistic aboriginal plain tribal group in Assam. Along with the Bodos, other ethnic communities like Adivasi, Bihari, Marwari, which have migrated from Central India, Bengali Muslim who have migrated from Bangladesh, Nepalis who have migrated from Nepal, and some indigenous communities of Assam like Koch Rajbonshi and Rabha reside in Bodoland along with the Bodos. Among the four districts of the BTAD region, the present study is conducted in Kokrajhar district. Kokrajhar is selected as it is the main headquarter of the BTAD region and Kokrajhar district covers the majority of the area, i.e 3165.44 sq. km in Bodoland. The region is also the hub of ethnic conflict in Western

Assam. According to 2011 Census, Kokrajhar has a total population of 8,86,999 persons. It has a population density of 280 per square kilometer. Kokrajhar has 3 sub-divisions, 11 Community Development Blocks, 5 Revenue Circles and 1068 villages. The present study is conducted in two villages of Gossaigaon sub-division of Kokrajhar district.

The Bodos consider themselves as the original inhabitants of the areas in the western part of Assam along the northern bank of Brahmaputra River. However, Bodos constitute only 46 per cent of the total population in BTR. The rest of the population consist of Bengali Muslims migrated from Bangladesh, Assamese and Bengali Hindus, Adivasis which were brought during the British rule from central India and the indigenous Assamese like Koch Rajbonshis and Rabhas. Bodos consider the other communities, especially the Bengali Muslim peasants and the Adivasis, as encroachers of their ancestral land and other resources. The eruption of frequent conflicts is triggered by the notion of dispossession of Bodoland by other communities. Thus, they started ethnic cleansing of those communities since 1993. Assam has witnessed several ethnic conflicts between the Bodos and the Santhals; and between the Bodos and the Bengali Muslims in 1993, 1996, 1998, 2008, 2012, 2014. Among the different ethnic conflicts in Bodoland, the conflict of 2012 was possibly India's worst case of mass human displacement where around 4,00,000 people were displaced from their homes. Thus, ethnic conflict in BTAD is reoccurring in nature and Kokrajhar being the main headquarter of the region is exposed to frequent ethnic conflicts.

Impact of Ethnic Conflict on Agriculture and Livelihood Activities

Ethnic conflicts have remained a major source of livelihood crisis in North-East India particularly in Assam. There is a close association between conflicts, violation of basic human rights, degradation of livelihood opportunities and endemic poverty which is becoming more evident by the reoccurring conflicts in Bodoland. During conflicts, the common people are the one who are targeted the most and are in effect the ones who suffer the most.

Agriculture is the main source of livelihood for the majority of the rural population in Kokrajhar district. Most of the villagers are engaged in agriculture and agriculture related activities as a means of livelihood. Ethnic conflicts in Bodoland had a negative impact on agriculture and have led to livelihood crises largely affecting the marginalized population of the villages. From the information collected through various sources, it was found that the conflict of 2012 affected the livelihood pattern of the victimized villages in Kokrajhar both directly and indirectly. During the conflict, there was a direct systematic attack on livelihood activities of both the communities involved in the conflict, i.e., Bengali Muslim and Bodo community. Both of the communities attacked each other's villages. Assets of the villagers including agricultural machinery, vehicles and food granaries were either looted or destroyed. The indirect affect was the systemic destruction of livelihood activities. During the conflict, the affected villagers were forced to flee from their villages and they had to stay in relief camps. Most of the displaced population was engaged in agricultural activities as a source of livelihood in their villages before the conflict. After displacement to relief camps, the farmers and agricultural labourers were unemployed for many months. Due to the destruction of agricultural assets during the conflict, villagers were financially incapable to be engaged in their previous source of income. In Table 8.1, the effect of the conflict on the loss of agricultural assets in shown.

Table 8.1: Effect of 2012 Conflict on Loss of Agricultural Assets in Babubil Village and Boro Binyakhata Village

Name of Assets	Assets in Babubil Village (%)		Assets in Binyakhata Village (%)	
	Before Conflict	After Conflict	Before Conflict	After Conflict
Poultry/pig	90	64	98	87
Cattle	82	68	88	80
Granary	76	54	92	88
Crops	80	66	96	92
Tractor	26	14	40	34
Power Tiller	8	2	16	12
Pickup Van	18	6	26	20
Thella	36	28	56	50

Source: Data collected from field survey.
Note: Figures in the table represents percentage to total.

From Table 8.1, it can been seen that among the 100 surveyed households of both the villages, almost everyone suffered loss of agricultural assets due to the 2012 conflict. During the conflict in Babubil village, all the surveyed households lost their crops and granary since it was burnt down by attackers and their livestock and agricultural machinery were stolen. After staying in refugee camps for 6 months, when they returned back to their village, many villagers did not have enough money to purchase new livestock and seeds to cultivate crops. Thus, we can see that after the conflict there has been a decrease in the percentage of people who owned poultry, cattle, granary, crops and agricultural machinery. In Binyakhata village, all the surveyed households suffered from agricultural loss during the conflict as they were temporarily displaced from their village for 3 months and their granary looted. There has been a reduction in the percentage of people who own agricultural assets after the conflict.

Since, most of the surveyed households were engaged in agricultural activities as a source of livelihood, after the conflict due to the pathetic financial situation, many had to change their source of income from agricultural activities to some other occupation. In Table 8.2, the changes in livelihood activities among the surveyed households are shown.

Table 8.2: Change in Livelihood Activities in Babubil Village and Boro Binyakhata Village

Livelihood Activity	Change in Babubil village (%)		Change in Binyakhata village (%)	
	Before Conflict	After Conflict	Before Conflict	After Conflict
Farmers	86	62	88	76
Agricultural Labourers	42	26	38	36
Animal Rearing	64	46	68	64
Small Enterprises	38	14	40	29
Vendors	10	45	28	35
Daily Wage Labourers	16	48	14	20
Household Workers	20	40	16	26
Govt. Employees	2	4	4	8

Source: Data collected from field survey.
Note: Figures in the table represents percentage to total.

From Table 8.2, it can be seen that majority of the population in the Babubil village was engaged in agricultural activities like farming, animal rearing and agricultural labourer before the conflict. Less percentage of people were engaged as vendors, daily wage labourers, and household workers but after the conflict, the number of people engaged in agricultural activities have decreased and more number of people started getting engaged as vendors, household workers or daily wage labourers as a source of livelihood.

In Boro Binyakhata village, most of the villagers were engaged in agricultural activities before the conflict and a small percentage of people were engaged as vendors, household labourers and daily wage labourers. From Table 8.2, it can be seen that, after the conflict though there has been a reduction in number of people engaged in agricultural activities, there is an increase in the number of vendors, daily wage labourers. However, people are still mostly engaged in agricultural related activities in the present day.

Due to the conflict period, agricultural activities were temporarily withheld which led to a reduction in production of foodgrains as well as non-foodgrains in Kokrajhar. From the secondary data collected from various government sources, it was found that production of both foodgrains as well as non-foodgrains decreased during the conflict years in Kokrajhar district, i.e., during the years 2012-2013 when major conflict took place between the Bodo and Muslims and again during the years 2014-2015 period when conflict took place between the Bodo and the Adivasi community.

Table 8.3: Area and Production for Foodgrains and Non-Foodgrains in Kokrajhar

Years	Foodgrains		Non-Foodgrains		Total Production of Grains
	Area	Production	Area	Production	
2010-11	120344	271382	4296	56714	328096
2011-12	129384	297256	5301	59784	357040
2012-13	100374	201226	2730	23810	225036
2013-14	121896	246732	3942	41341	288073
2014-15	110921	206987	3406	33576	240563
2015-16	148156	524356	5369	41096	565452
2016-17	148877	1002276	5625	60248	1062524

Source: Data collected from Statistical Handbook of BTAD, Assam.
Note: *Area = Hectare, Production = Mega tonne.
*Figures in the parentheses represent percentage to total.

The figures in Table 8.3 are represented in the form of diagram in Fig. 8.1. Fig. 8.1 shows the total production of Grains including both Foodgrain and Non-Foodgrains in Kokrajhar district during the years 2010 to 2017. From Fig. 8.1, it can be seen that, during the years 2012-2013 the total production of Grains reduced to a great extent. During 2013-2014, the total production of grains increased to some extent and again in the years 2014-2015, there was a reduction in the production of grains. After 2015, there is a gradual increase in the total quantity of grains produced in the region. During the two major conflicts which occurred during 2012 and 2014, there was a reduction in the total production of grains in Kokrajhar District. Thus, conflict affected agricultural activity of the region to a great extent.

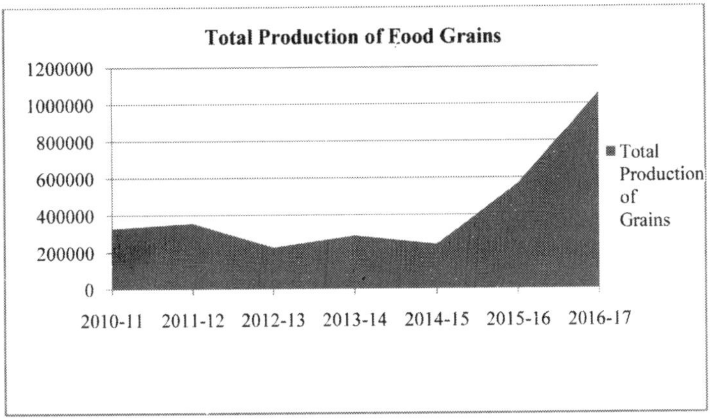

Fig. 8.1: Total Production of Foodgrains in Kokrajhar District in Different Years.

Conclusion

From the study it can be seen that Ethnic Conflict has had a devastating impact on the life of the rural population in Kokrajhar. Conflicts have led to a decrease in agricultural production due to the loss of agricultural assets and the degraded financial condition during the conflict. This has resulted in changes in the livelihood activities among many of the affected population of both the surveyed villages. Conflict has contributed to acceleration in poverty of the area. In a myriad of ways, ethnic conflicts have acted as a barrier preventing the sustainable rural development of Kokrajhar. Thus, the government should take the required steps to prevent the reoccurrence of ethnic conflict in Kokrajhar.

REFERENCES

Addison, T., Chowdhury, A.R., & Murshed, S.M. (2002). *By how much does conflict reduce financial development?* (No. 2002/48). WIDER Discussion Paper.

Baruah, A.K. (1991). *Social tensions in Assam: Middle class politics.* Purbanchal Prakash.

Baruah, S. (2003). Citizens and denizens: Ethnicity, homeland and the crisis of displacement in Northeast India. *Journal of Refugee Studies*, *16*(1), 44-66.

Bennett, O., Bexley, J., & Warnock, K. (1995). Arms to protect, arms to fight: *Women speak out about conflict.* London: Panos, 290.

Das, S.K. (2012). Socio-Economic Empowerment of Women through SHG-Banking Linkage Programme: A Boon for Development. *International Journal of Management & Business Studies*, *2*(1), 39-46.

Gardam, J. (1997). Women and the law of armed conflict: why the silence? *International & Comparative Law Quarterly*, *46*(1), 55-80.

Hussain, Monirul. (2000). State, identity movements and internal displacement in the North-East. *Economic and Political Weekly*, *51*(35), 4519-4523.

M.P. Banton, Ethnicity, Ethnic Groups, in Michael Mann, ed., *Macmillan Student Encyclopedia of Sociology*. Macmillan.

Swargiary, Noas. (1997). The Bodo mass movements since independence. In Thomas Pulloppillil and Jacob Aluckal (Eds.), *The Bodos: children of bhullum butter*. 78-98. Spectrum Publishers.

Young, H., Aklilu, Y., Were, G., Catley, A., Leyland, T., Borrel, A., Roberts, A.R., Webb, P., Holland, D., Johnecheck, W. and Jacobsen, K. (2002) *Nutrition and Livelihoods in Situations of Conflict and other Crises*. Medford, Massachusetts, USA: Feinstein International Famine Center, Tufts University.

Section IV

9
The Naga Story of Conflict

Kethoser (Aniu) Kevichusa

During the last several decades, the Nagas have been embroiled in one of the world's longest nationalist conflicts that has claimed thousands of lives (Ayres, 2000; Baruah, 2003; Franke, 2006). The Naga conflict originally began as a struggle for Naga independence, and initially displayed remarkable Naga solidarity founded upon romantic idealism. It has, however, long since degenerated into a cycle of factional feuds that has caught Naga society in the vortex of hatred, violence, and vengeance. This chapter briefly retraces the history of the Naga conflict, highlighting its historical, geographical, and political contours by using John Paul Lederach's analysis of deeply divided societies as a lens for looking into the conflict.

The Naga Story

The Nagas are a group of several tribes[1] who occupy a contiguous tract of mountainous territory between India and Myanmar.[2] In India, they are found in the north-eastern Indian states of Nagaland, Manipur, Assam, and Arunachal Pradesh; in Myanmar, they are found in Sagaing Division and Kachin state.[3] While it is difficult to give a precise official number to the actual Naga population, it is estimated that it is between 3.5 and 4 million (Baruah, 2003). The population of the state of Nagaland is approximately 2 million.

Prior to the dawn of the twentieth century, it can be argued that there was no self-conscious or intentional 'Naga identity' as such. People did not identify themselves beyond their particular village or tribe. Each village was a sort of sovereign republic and different tribes had different polities. Their small world was, on the one hand, one of internecine headhunting feuds among themselves – whether inter-village or inter-tribal – and with their neighbours in the plains; and, on the other, one that every now and again evidenced remarkable solidarity in the face of a common enemy. The absence of a self-conscious concept of Naga identity and nationality until recently, is often used as an argument against the pan-Naga nationalistic project. Baruah, for example, argues powerfully that the Naga nationalist movement is a classic case of 'constructionism' that lacks historical basis and collides with other projects of identity construction, not least that of their neighbours' identity constructions (Baruah, 2003).

About 90 per cent of Nagas are also Baptist Christians. Christianity first came to the Nagas through the American Baptist missionaries in the second half of the nineteenth century, but the massive conversions took place only after the independence movement gained momentum.[4]

While many trace the beginnings of the Naga conflict to the early part of the twentieth century, Nagas, nationalists and others, claim that the roots of the conflict can be found in the first and most direct colonial action to affect the Nagas, namely, the Treaty of Yandabo of 1826. The Naga claim is that this Anglo-Burmese treaty severed Naga country and the Naga people without their knowledge, with one-half falling under Burma and the other half falling on the Indian side that makes up present-day Northeast India. Following this event, the British made a number of expeditions against the Nagas that were fiercely resisted by the Naga tribes. In 1866-67, the British set up a headquarter in Naga territory as their 'first permanent footing' (Reid, 1983 [1942], p. 99). In 1879-1880, after a bloody battle, the last organised Naga resistance to the British fell, and the Nagas officially came under the British administration. The British thus made the Naga Hills a British district in 1881 (Reid, 1983 [1942], p. 99). There were, however, many Naga areas in the east that were not administered by the British. These were called the 'un-administered areas' by the British.

The actual emergence of the 'Naga national consciousness' can be traced to 1918, when a handful of Nagas came together and formed the 'Naga Club'. In the late 1920s, with the possibility of the British leaving India arising, the Nagas also seriously began considering the possibility of Naga independence (Chasie, 1999, p. 26). In 1929, when the Indian Statutory Commission, dispatched for the study of constitutional reforms in India and led by Sir John Simon, visited the Naga Hills, the Naga Club – claiming to represent the tribes to which they belonged – presented a memorandum to the Commission, which came to be known as the 1929 Simon Commission Memorandum. The Memorandum stated that before the British conquered Naga country, the Assamese of the Assam Valley to the north and the Manipuris in the south had "never conquered us nor were we subjected to their rule". While it conceded that "We have no unity among us and it is really the British Government that is holding us together now", it also pleaded, "If the British Government, however, wants to throw us away, we pray that we should not be thrust to the mercy of the people who could never subjugate us, but to leave us alone to determine for ourselves as in ancient times" (Simon Commission Memorandum, 1929 [1999]).

The Government of India Act, 1935, which was the outcome of the Commission's report, put the Naga Hills under what the Act called 'Excluded Areas' that were left directly under the British Crown's Representative. Nagas took this to be of great significance, taking it to imply a kind of special provision or arrangement that excluded the Naga Hills from the rest of India. Elwin, however, says that such an interpretation was unwarranted:

> There seems to be an impression that the members of the Commission were so impressed by the Naga claims that they made some special arrangement to exclude the Nagas from the proposed reforms. In actual fact, as we have seen, this was not so. There was no special arrangement for the Naga Hills District and the fact that it was classified as an Excluded Area simply brought it into line with a number of similar areas throughout the whole of India. (Elwin, 1961, p. 50)

In April 1945, with the departure of the British from India imminent, the Naga Hills District Tribal Council, comprising representative tribal councils from various tribes, was formed. This Council replaced the earlier Naga Club. In 1946, this Council became the Naga National Council (NNC), which became the umbrella political organisation for the struggle for Naga independence.

From 26 to 28 June, 1947, discussions were held between the Government of India (GoI), represented by the then Governor of Assam Sir Akbar Hydari, and representatives of the NNC. The outcome of these discussions later came to be known as the Nine Point Agreement or Hydari Agreement. The Agreement granted far-reaching autonomy to the NNC. It recognised the right of the Nagas to freely develop themselves according to their own wishes, and handed the affairs of the Naga Hills – judicial, executive, legislative, land, and taxation – to the NNC. The agreement also guaranteed "to bring under one unified administrative unit as far as possible all Nagas" (The Hydari Agreement, 1947). It was, however, the ninth point that proved problematic. It said:

> The Governor of Assam as the Agent of the Government of the Indian Union will have a special responsibility for a period of 10 years to ensure the observance of the agreement, at the end of this period, the Naga Council will be asked whether they require the above agreement to be extended for a further period or a new agreement regarding the future of Naga people arrived at. (The Hydari Agreement, 1947)

The Nagas interpreted this clause as granting them the right to self-determination, including the right to be independent, at the end of the ten-year period. The Indian side denied this, and the Constituent Assembly of India refused to ratify it. In July 1947, a Naga delegation met with Mahatma Gandhi, where Gandhi is reported to have said:

> We do not want the British and they are going. If you say that you are not Indians and your country does not belong to India, then the matter ends there. Nobody will force you to join the Indian Union (Kevichusa, 1995).

There was, however, no significant progress in the understanding between the incoming Indian Government and the NNC. Thus, on 14 August, 1947, a day before the Indian declaration of independence, the NNC declared independence. India ignored the declaration. In 1950, A.Z. Phizo, also known as 'the father of Naga nationalism', was elected NNC President, and the Naga independence movement gained momentum with the launching of a campaign of civil non-cooperation with India. On 16 May, 1951, a plebiscite conducted by the NNC claimed that 99 per cent of Nagas supported independence. The next year Nagas boycotted the first Indian general election. The

GoI responded by banning the NNC and issuing arrest warrants against its leaders who went underground. In March 1953, the Indian Prime Minister, Nehru, and his Burmese counterpart, U Nu, came to Kohima (which is today the capital town of Nagaland). This event, however, took an unfortunate turn when the Nagas leaders were refused – perhaps without Nehru's own knowledge – a meeting with the Prime Minister or to submit any memoranda. In response, the Naga public of about 4,000 people staged a walkout from the public meeting that had been arranged: ' "If he will not listen to us, why should we listen to him' was the prompt Naga reaction" (Chasie, 1999, p. 40). The event, rccounted by Mullik, the then Director of the Indian Intelligence Bureau, is as amusing as it is tragic:

> [B]y the time the Prime Minister arrived and ascended the rostrum along with U Nu, the entire Naga audience excepting a few government servants left the place of the meeting. I had been to innumerable public meetings with the Prime Minister and he in his life had addressed thousands of meetings attended sometimes by well over a million people; this was probably the first time when a public meeting to be addressed by Pandit Nehru, the darling of India's crowds, to hear and see whom people would trudge scores of miles, was effectively boycotted and he was left to address a few dozens of Government servants and their family members, most of whom were not Nagas but plains people. The Prime Minister was shocked. So was U Nu. We could not talk. We came back to the DC's house where sumptuous food awaited us but none had any appetite. (Mullik, 1972, p. 305)

It is tragic because this was a very significant visit that turned into a debacle. A settlement of the Naga problem would have to involve the Governments of India and Burma, and here were both the leaders of the two nations in person. According to Chasie, "At this initial stage too, Nehru and U Nu could have settled the Naga problem between them without too much difficulty, given the required political will on their part" (Chasie, 1999, pp. 39-40). It is also said that Nehru never forgot the insult.

In September 1954, Phizo declared the formation of the People's Sovereign Republic of Free Nagaland. Soon after that, the movement took a violent turn. According to Mullik, "Troops moved into Tuensang [a Naga area] by October 1955, and the war with Nagas started from then" (Mullik, 1972, p. 308). In 1956, the NNC formed the Naga Central Government – renamed the Federal Government of Nagaland (FGN) in 1959 – and its own 'army'. From what initially began as opportunistic guerrilla warfare between the world's largest standing army and a band of rag-tag guerrillas drawing their sustenance from public support, the conflict soon flared up and caught the whole Naga civilian population in its wake.

During this time, there was nearly one security troop member for every adult male Naga in the Naga areas (Mullik, 1972, pp. 313-314). The Indian armed forces were armed and protected with legislations enacted and promulgated by the Indian Parliament such as The Assam Maintenance of Public Order (Autonomous Districts) Act, 1953, The Assam Disturbed Areas Act, 1955, and The Armed Forces (Special Powers) Act, 1958 (AFSPA). These Acts effectively gave the Indian armed forces unrestricted power to carry out their military operations in the Naga areas without any political or legal interference. The AFSPA, which remains in force to this day, not only grants sweeping powers to the armed forces to destroy property, search premises, and make arrests without warrant, but also empowers even a non-commissioned army officer to "fire upon or otherwise use force, even to the causing of death", any person on mere suspicion (The Armed Forces [Special Powers] Act, 1958). The Act also guarantees that legal action cannot be taken against members of the Indian armed forces for anything done, or purported to be done, under the Act, without the sanction of the GoI. Protected by such legislation, human rights violations became rampant and routine: "People were brutalized, women raped, villages burnt and churches defiled" (Burman, 2008, p. 150). Iralu says that between 1955 and 1956, the Indian security forces burnt down more than 645 out of approximately 860 Naga villages existing in those days (Iralu, 2000, p. 99). While it is impossible to give an exact number, deaths from shooting, torture, starvation and other brutalities would number – even by the most conservative estimates and after reading the nationalists' estimates against the grain – in the thousands. According to Linyü, between 1956 and 1958, 591 people from the Angami tribe alone were shot dead or tortured to death (Linyü, 2004, p. 123).

When the violent conflict with India began, rifts among the Nagas, including within the NNC itself, began to emerge. On the one side were the extremist group within the NNC who took a more confrontational approach with regard to the Naga problem, and who were by this time gaining influence and ascendancy. On the other side were the moderate group who had hitherto adopted and advocated a non-violent approach based on political negotiations and parleys with the Indian side. The more militant group thus began threatening and killing the moderates who disagreed with the confrontational stance that they were adopting and also those Nagas who were serving under the GoI. During this time, a prominent Naga leader and architect of Naga nationalism, T. Sakhrie, who advocated a non-violent, political approach for Naga nationalism was brutally killed by the hard line nationalists.

In 1957, a 'Naga People's Convention' (NPC) was held. The Convention leaders comprised Naga moderates and included former underground members who had come overground. The Convention was also supposed to "act as a via media between the government of India and Naga rebels" (Alemchiba, 1970, p. 186). After holding another Convention in 1958, however, representatives of the NPC got into negotiations with the GoI towards the formation of a state within the Indian Union. Although there were a number of prominent NPC leaders who objected to this dubious move and resigned from the NPC, a 16-point memorandum was prepared by the NPC and agreed with the GoI. Thus, on 1 December, 1963, the state of Nagaland was declared as the sixteenth state within the Indian Union. The NNC refused to recognise statehood as they considered it a significant setback to its call to independence. Thus, rather than quell the nationalist movement, it intensified intra-Naga political rivalries and complicated the Naga political landscape. According to Goswami, "With statehood, inter-tribal rivalry that plagues Nagaland till date increased and clashes between pro-Phizo and pro-statehood groups, interspersed by tribal differences, intensified" (Goswami, 2007, p. 294). The main leader of the NPC, Dr. Imkongliba Ao, was promptly killed by the NNC/FGN – another symbolic political killing in the Naga spiral into violence.

A significant progress towards peace in Nagaland was made in 1964. By this time, "The Nagas' desire for Peace was as deep, if not deeper, as their desire for freedom" (Linyü, 2004, p. 149). Through the endeavour of the Nagaland Baptist Church Council (NBCC) and the Peace Mission it had set up, representatives of the FGN and the GoI signed an armistice treaty, The Cease Fire Agreement, in August 1964.

The Agreement, which came into effect at midnight 5/6 September, 1964, was also meant to lead to peace talks between the FGN and the GoI. Thanksgiving services were held in every town and village in Nagaland. To this day, 6 September is commemorated as Nagaland Peace Day.

A number of things, however, led to the collapse of the Agreement in 1972. First of all, there were allegations and counter-allegations of violations of the terms of the Agreement between the FGN and the GoI. Second, internal political wrangles, rifts, and betrayals led to a split within the FGN along tribal lines. Third, during this time another key dissenter and Naga army war hero, General Kaito, was killed by the NNC/FGN. The wounds of these events remain unresolved and unhealed. Fourth, after the failed assassination of the then Chief Minister of Nagaland, Hokishe, by the FGN, the GoI banned the NNC, the FGN and the Naga Army. Finally, the GoI unilaterally withdrew from the Agreement in 1972. Hostilities resumed, and Nagaland was once again plunged into another episode of violence.[5]

A major political development took place in 1975. On 11 November, 1975, a treaty known as the Shillong Accord was signed between the Governor, representing the GoI, and certain 'representatives of the underground organisations' (Shillong Accord, 1975). This Accord was to prove to be yet another contentious – perhaps even the most – issue in Naga politics. Although the Accord was signed under the terrible pressure of Indian army brutality and Naga public attrition, it included the unconditional acceptance of the Constitution of India. The agreement confused the Naga public and fractured the Naga movement. While the official NNC distanced itself from the Accord – neither condemning it nor endorsing it – some leading underground members condemned it as a treacherous sell-out. These nationalists broke away from the NNC because Phizo, who had by then fled to and settled in London but remained NNC President, remained silent on the issue despite several pleas from them to denounce it. Thus, 1980 saw the formation of the National Socialist Council of Nagaland (NSCN).[6] This group was led by Th. Muivah, Isak Swu and S.S. Khaplang. Since then, "The Accordists, as they came to be called, were, literally, hounded by those who opposed it and several killed" (Chasie, 1999, p. 43). The gulf between the so-called 'Accordists' and the 'Non-accordists' remain as wide as ever, and has claimed the lives of many.

The NSCN further split in 1988 into the NSCN-Isak-Muivah (NSCN-IM) faction and the NSCN-Khaplang (NSCN-K) faction. In 1990, Phizo passed away in London. His passing away led to further divisions within the original NNC. Currently, in addition to the Nagaland state government that functions under the purview of the Indian constitution, there are several nationalist groups, divided along ideological and (partly) tribal lines, each running its own parallel government. Writing in 1999, Chasie says:

> Factional fights became a regular feature and many, including non-factional and innocent Nagas, have died at the hands of fellow-Nagas who claim to be Naga Nationalists! Factional rivalry also resulted, in certain cases, in the signing up of criminal elements, whose ideals could not have been as lofty as their predecessors, and, sometimes, leading to the break-down in the chains of command. (Chasie, 1999, p. 43)

In 1997, the NSCN-IM signed a ceasefire agreement with the GoI. The NSCN-K also followed with a ceasefire agreement with the GoI. These ceasefire agreements have so far been renewed periodically. And whilst they have drastically brought down the conflict level between nationalists and the Indian armed forces (for statistics, see Singh, 2007), they have, however, resulted in the brazen conduct of the nationalists in public life: institutionalised extortion, kidnappings, targeted killings, and all-out factional battles in public areas have become part of everyday life in Nagaland. The NSCN-K further split in 2008 into the NSCN-Unification and the NSCN-K. Since then, there have yet been more splits of the factions.

Anatomy of Deeply Divided Societies

In his book, *Building Peace: Sustainable Reconciliation in Divided Societies* (Lederach, 1997), Lederach delineates what he calls 'characteristics of deeply divided societies'. By the phrase 'deeply divided societies', Lederach refers to societies that are experiencing 'armed conflicts'.[7] Lederach begins his discussion by highlighting several starting points for considering such societies. Lederach says that (a) ideological paradigms that are relevant for understanding international conflicts are often inapplicable for most contemporary conflicts; (b) the vast majority of armed conflicts take place in the developing world; (c) most of these conflicts are intranational in scope, that is, they are between groups within the boundaries of a defined state; (d) although these conflicts may be intranational, they internationalise to the degree that some participants, especially opposition movements, inhabit neighbouring countries, weaponry and financial assistance flow in from surrounding or more distant regions, and refugees cross national borders; (e) such conflicts contribute to regional – not just national – instability and conflict; and (f) the easy availability of light weaponry with which these conflicts are mostly fought contributes to the volatility and the capacity of the conflictants over long periods.

Having highlighted these observations, Lederach identifies four factors that interact in deeply divided societies. The first is the 'narrowing of identities'. In societies of armed conflicts, cohesion, and identity tend to form along increasingly narrow lines than those of national citizenship. This narrowing is caused by deep and long-standing roots of distrust and fear coupled with immediate experiences of violence, atrocities, and division. Geography also plays an important role in narrowing of identities. Because intranational conflicts, unlike international conflict, take place in localised contexts, the immediacy of the conflict is felt all the more, with the result that people seek security and identity in increasingly smaller groups. The unit of identity and cohesion may be the clan, ethnicity, religion, geographic/regional affiliation, or a mix of all these. While ideology and class are often not the lines along which identities are drawn in most contemporary conflict, they are often underlying forces that leaders of conflicting groups exploit for domination and control. One of the consequences of a narrowing of identities is a breakdown of centralised authority (and, sometimes, of state infrastructure).

The second (twofold) characteristic of deeply divided societies is directly related to the first, and they are: factionalism and diffusion of power. A recurring complexity of most intranational contemporary conflicts is the multiplicity of groups or factions, each vying for power and control. The rapid creation of new groups, the shifting of alliances, and the autonomy of action within groups and subgroups, means that in contexts of conflict, power is diffuse (i.e., lacking clarity) and in contrast to more stable societies where power issues out of a statist hierarchy of one sort or another. The consequence of this diffusion of power is, first, that the command and control of individual leaders over their respective groups and their actions is never easy to assess; and, second, establishing appropriate mechanisms of representation and decision-making for the population becomes extremely difficult.

A third characteristic of deeply divided societies is that the conflicts that these societies find themselves caught in are often protracted and intractable. This means that the perceptions and stereotyping, animosity, fear, and hatred among groups are deep-rooted, passing from one generation to another. When this long-standing nature of these conflicts is coupled with the sense of vulnerability that proximity with and immediacy of the enemy generates, a dynamic of socio-psychological perceptions, emotions, and subjective experiences that have little to do with substantive original differences or issues begins to drive and sustain the conflict. Over time, conflict comes to be accepted by all parties involved as the way of group survival and self-preservation, and not as something that is oppressive and detrimental to all involved.

The fourth characteristic of most intranational contemporary conflicts is the absence or limited availability of formal governmental or international mechanisms for dealing with the conflict. The founding charters of key international organisations, such as the United Nations Organisation (UNO), lay out strict limitations against intervention in the internal affairs of its member-states. Moreover, the traditional paradigms of these organisations in approaching conflicts remain limited to international, statist diplomacy. Thus, given that most of these conflicts are internal or intranational by nature, recourse to resolving conflicts through international bodies becomes very limited.

The Nagas: A Typical Case of Deeply Divided Societies

The Naga conflict is a case where Lederach's analysis of a deeply divided society applies more or less completely. All the starting points highlighted by Lederach can be illustrated by the Naga conflict: It is taking place in the developing world; it is intranational in scope, in the sense that the conflict is located within the boundaries of a defined state (namely, India and/or Burma); that it has been internationalised in the sense that many of the conflictants have their bases in and operate out of neighbouring regions (such as Burma, Bangladesh, and Nepal), weaponry and other assistance flow in from neighbouring and more distant nations (such as China and Pakistan), and that the conflict has been a major contributor to the instability of the region.

More importantly, Lederach's four characteristics of deeply divided societies precisely articulate the predicament of contemporary Naga society. First, the conflict is marked by an ever-narrowing of identities. The Naga conflict began with the idealistic assertion of a 'Naga identity' that was distinct from and opposed to Indian national citizenship. It was thus a formation and assertion of identity narrower than that of Indian national citizenship. As the conflict progressed, due to deep traditional roots of intra-Naga enmity and distrust, and contemporary experiences of manipulation, violence, atrocities, and division, there has been an ever-increasing tendency towards (a return to) smaller groups and subgroups. Ideological and political groups, whether they are the underground nationalists or the 'overground' state political parties and actors, are also increasingly along narrow tribal affiliations. Thus, for example, among the nationalist groups, the NNC is predominated by the Angami, Chakesang, and Khiamnungam tribes, the NSCN (I-M) by the Tangkhul and Sumi tribes, the NSCN (K) by the Konyaks.

Factionalism is one of the biggest problems besetting Naga society. The phenomenon, besides terribly complicating the Indo-Naga political issue, has become a scourge in day-to-day Naga life. What began as one national movement for independence under the NNC has now fragmented into at least half a dozen different factions, all armed and vying for domination and control. Added to this are the various tribal organisations and other public bodies, each claiming to 'represent' 'the people'. The consequence of this is a confused diffusion of power and the absence of an effective centralised authority. This, in turn, means that the different groups and subgroups become unaccountable and autonomous in their actions. It also means that decision-making processes for the general population becomes extremely difficult and decisions made are often ineffective. To be sure, in recent years, there has been considerable decline in all out violent conflict, whether at the Indo-Naga level or the intra-Naga level. But historically-felt fear, animosity, hatred, and suspicion among the various groups and tribes are being passed on from generation to generation. Peace in the land of the Nagas remains an elusive dream.

NOTES

1. The Indian census lists 35 Naga tribes living in India.
2. Although I am aware of the different political connotations in the uses of 'Burma' and 'Myanmar', in this work I use them interchangeably.
3. It is, in this connection, important to be aware that when one speaks of Nagas, one is not necessarily referring only to the Nagas of the Indian state of Nagaland inhabited only by 17 Naga tribes, but also a 'pan-Naga identity' spread over a 'pan-Naga territory'.
4. For a study paralleling the Naga independence movement and the Naga church movement, see Linyü, 2004.
5. The response of the public to the collapse of the Cease Fire Agreement was poignant. From 2 to 6 September, 1972, thousands of people from all over Nagaland came to Kohima, the capital town, and took turns to ring a huge church bell once every five minutes, through night and day, for five continuous days. During those five days, people wore black armbands and vehicles flew black flags. In the afternoon of the last day, a large stone was taken to the heart of Kohima and ceremoniously buried. This five-day dramatic episode was the Naga people's mournful response to the breakdown of the ceasefire. The tolling of the bell, the black cloths, and the burial of the stone symbolised the death and burial of Peace in Nagaland (Linyü, 2004, pp. 1-2).
6. The NSCN-IM later changed the 'Nagaland' in their organisation's name to 'Nagalim' (lim in the Ao language means 'land') because of the political connotation of the term 'Nagaland' which has come to be closely associated with the Indian state of Nagaland formed in 1963.
7. 'Armed conflict' is a categorisation widely used by researchers to refer to conflict at one of the three levels – minor armed conflict, intermediate armed conflict, and war (Wallensteen & Axell, 1993).

REFERENCES

Alemchiba, M. (1970). *A Brief Historical Account of Nagaland.* Kohima: Naga Institute of Culture.

Ayres, R.W. (2000). A World Flying Apart? Violent Nationalist Conflict and the End of the Cold War. *Journal of Peace Research, 37*(1), 105-117.

Baruah, S. (2003). Confronting Constructionism: Ending India's Naga War. *Journal of Peace Research, 40*(3), 321-338.

Burman, J.J.R. (2008). Contours of the Naga Upsurge. *AEJ, 6*, 145-156.

Chasie, C. (1999). *The Naga Imbroglio: A Personal Perspective.* Kohima: Standard Printers and Publishers.

Elwin, V. (1961). *Nagaland.* Shillong: P. Dutta for the Research Department, Adviser's Secretariat, Shillong.

Franke, M. (2006). Wars without End: The Case of the Naga Hills. *Diogenes, 212*, 69-84.

Goswami, N. (2007). The Naga Narrative of Conflict: Envisioning a Resolution Roadmap. *Strategic Analysis, 31*(2), 287-313.

Iralu, K. (2000). *Nagaland and India: The Blood and the Tears*: Publisher Unknown.

Kevichusa, T.P. (1995). *Address by the General Secretary of Naga National Council on the Occasion of Gandhi Jayanti Day at Kewhira.*

Lederach, J. P. (1997). *Building Peace: Sustainable Reconciliation in Divided Societies*. Washington, DC: United States Institute of Peace Press.

Linyü, K. (2004). *Christian Movements in Nagaland.* Kohima: N.V. Press.

Mullik, B.N. (1972). *My Years with Nehru 1948-1964*. New Delhi: Allied Publishers.

Reid, S.R. (1983 [1942]). *History of the frontier areas bordering on Assam (From 1883-1941*). Delhi: Eastern Publishing House.

Simon Commission Memorandum. (1929 [1999]). Memorandum of the Naga Hills to Simon Commission. In *The Naga Imbroglio* (pp. 165-167). Kohima: Standard Printers and Publishers.

Singh, G. (2007). A Decade of Ceasefire in Nagaland. *Strategic Analysis, 31*(5), 815-832.

The Armed Forces [Special Powers] Act (1958). The Armed Forces (Special Powers) Act, 1958. Retrieved from http://www.satp.org/satporgtp/countries/india/document/actandordinances/armed_forces_special_power_act_1958.htm

The Hydari Agreement. (1947). The Naga-Akbar Hydari Accord, 1947. Retrieved from http://www.satp.org/satporgtp/countries/india/states/nagaland/documents/papers/nagaland_9point.htm

Wallensteen, P., & Axell, K. (1993). Armed Conflict at the End of the Cold War, 1989-92. *Journal of Peace Research, 30*(3), 331-346. Retrieved from http://www.jstor.org/stable/424810

10

The Khasi Indigenous Beliefs and Christianity

An Encounter or a Negotiation?

Ruth Ibameri Kharbamon

The world today is characterized by a rapid blurring and blending of cultures. Cultural boundaries have become increasingly blurred for cultures have become both more globalised and also more fragmented and de-centred. The relentless process of globalization has made in-roads even into the distant and remote hill State of Meghalaya. Camouflaged with the spread of trade and cultural exchange in the name of development, globalization has manifested itself and has gained phenomenal in-roads in the state. The diffusion of Western values, consumer goods and lifestyles has affected the identity of the hill tribes through a neglect of whatever is local or traditional. To have an identity is to have features that are both relevant and enduring. Today, the local tribal cultures, if not careful, are in the process of slowly and steadily sliding away into cultural irrelevance in a fast-changing scientifically advanced world, losing out on their fantasized traditions and beliefs.

The chapter briefly highlights some of the forces which have led to this state of affairs and attempts to understand the relationship that exists between the indigenous traditional faith of the Khasis and Christianity, which in a way has initiated the process of globalization of thought, spiritual and social practices.

The pre-colonial Khasi tribe existed with a social, cultural and political system of their own. They had their birth naming ceremonies, their ancestor worship, folktales or folk stories, their bone collection rituals and their megalithic culture. There were legends, myths and tales, dances and choral chanting. They had an identity that could be called their own. However, the process of change in the Khasi society began with the British and their annexation of the Khasi Hills in 1833. With the Charter Act of 1813 which allowed the Protestant Missions to preach the Gospel in India, the Baptist Missionaries of Serampore were the earliest to extend their activities to the North-East Frontier. Krishna Pal, the first convert of William Carey was indeed the first missionary to the Khasis and the North East. He propagated the Gospel among the Khasis in their own vernacular, using the Bengali script (Syiemlieh, 2013: 36).

The mission work was carried on by Alexander Lish, but because of his ill health, he had to leave Cherrapunji in 1883. The evangelization process was left to Thomas Jones of the Welsh Presbyterian mission who, through his sustained labour and untiring zeal, managed to bring about a transformation and enduring mark on the religious, educational and social and cultural life of the tribes. Though the initial purpose of Jones and his colleagues was to preach the Christian conception of salvation, they also brought with them Western values and culture which were to leave a lasting mark in the life of the Khasis. The use of the Roman script to preach and teach the people also laid the landmark in the history of the evolution of the tribe. Hence, urbanization, new administrative orientations, the emergence of new trade structures and social contacts, culminated in bringing about a radical social and cultural transformation. The changes no doubt eradicated to a great extent the practices and customs of sorcery and superstitious beliefs but at the same time, they brought in a totally new worldview in the spiritual and emotional beliefs of the indigenous Khasi tribe, challenging the very foundation of their previous notion of themselves.

Bareh in his *The History and Culture of the Khasi People* highlighted the impact of the British missionaries among the tribes when he says:

> Christians no longer observe their old religious beliefs and rituals... In Christian areas, old practices of megalithic erections, community religious celebrations and festivals have become obliterated. Christianity has caused reversals in marriages, naming, funerals, house building and village ceremonies... connoting abandonment of the old religious faith and belief. With them several social festivities, sport games and other aspects of cultural heritage have also been forgotten. (Bareh 1985: 405)

When the old rites and rituals became disused, the singing of folk songs suffered too. Earlier no occasion was complete or meaningful unless accompanied by the lore of folk songs and choral chanting. The themes of the songs are varied. They talk of war and peace, prowess of heroic characters and legendary lovers. This abandonment of folk singing among the Khasi converts contributed to the decline of what would otherwise have been interesting traditional practices.

The transformation through proselytization brought about a renewed mind-set and the attachment Khasis had to their roots was there but the relevance and interpretation changed. With a change of spirituality also came a change of meaning. Unlike the other tribes of the North East where even Christian converts are very much part of the cultural and traditional ceremonies and festivities, a serious drawback among the Khasi community is the misunderstanding that exists till date between the Khasi Christians and those still holding the indigenous Khasi faith. It is worth mentioning here that the Christian way of living which is followed in the neighbouring states of Nagaland and Mizoram is different from what was proposed by the first missionaries. Unlike the Khasis, the Mizos and Nagas have not forfeited their tribes' main festivities. Traditional dances and songs continue to be a part of their lives and Christians are a part of all festivities ranging from the State's Day to the Baptist centenary celebrations. This unfortunately does not happen among the Khasis and Jaintias. The participation of the Khasi Christians in the traditional festivals has often been discouraged.

The present generation of Khasis is beset with questions of identity and relevance. The academic curriculum as well as social practices has of late relegated into the background issues and discourses related to culture. Khasi folk songs and dance have not been popularized in a manner that would be befitting of a thriving tribal society. This is predominantly more significant with the Khasi diaspora. The export of culture has not happened simultaneously with the migration of the people. The identity has no doubt been respectably maintained in terms of conventional practices like matrilineal lineage or the familial connection, but due to the challenges of location and resources, Khasi folk songs or dance or even food have their limitations. Media and political development have not been used to its full potential in the Khasi society in comparison to other society. Even the vernacular and printing press was not used which the present generation lack the knowledge and quality understanding of its own culture and identity.

For instance, other societies take their culture very seriously such as the Bengalis, the Assamese and the Tamils. We can see that their culture and identity is beaming in Television sets twenty-four hours a day. Songs and dances always have that cultural essence connected to folklore, when it was played in movies and short videos. The masses have that nostalgia feeling and a feeling of belonging of the past when they listen to it, connecting with their own ancestors. The Khasi language still has a long way to go from being recognized as one of the official languages of India. Presently, serious efforts are being made by the political representatives of the State for the inclusion of the Khasi language into the Eighth Schedule of the Constitution of India. The move is genuine. It certainly is a good move. But the question is – Is that all? More than this, the Khasis will have to be aware of their identity – they should know where they come from and who they are. They should be familiar with their culture, their tradition and their roots so that they can be in every sense a Khasi, with a unique identity, and with a deep sense of belonging to the community. In a globalized world, it will be a tremendous challenge to the present generation with diffusion and assimilation playing an important part. If they are not rooted to a firm ground, then they are liable to be influenced or invaded by other cultures, especially to the ones that reside outside the peripheral of its own area and society.

The missionaries had done much to help enlighten the hill people by conferring upon them the benefits of an education that was rooted in the western scientific model. They ushered in rational thinking, scientific temper and encouraged a mind-set of growth through their educational and spiritual interventions. This was the policy adopted by Thomas Jones. He wanted to educate the Khasi first and then, to evangelize the tribes gradually. "The only plan which appears to me likely to answer a good purpose", he observed, "is to establish schools in the various villages to teach the Khasi children and adults to read their own languages and to instruct them in the principle of the Christian religion. In this way we shall not only bring up the young people in the knowledge of the gospel doctrines but we shall also teach them to read" (Jyrwa, 2011:96). This according to Jones was an important step towards the evangelization of the tribes. The establishment of schools and the adoption of the Roman script had a major impact on the psyche of the people. In fact, the self-service and dedication of the missionaries won the hearts of the people so much so that the Khasis openly expressed their keen desire of learning the language of '*U Dohlieh*,' 'the white man' and adopting their way of life.

While a change was certainly affected and the transformation was phenomenal, and it cannot be denied the missionaries' contribution towards the education and socio development of the tribes. A notable Church historian once remarked that, "Christianity is the story of how it lifted and gave a sense of dignity, equality and identity to the so-called backward classes, the lower castes and the untouchables of the Indian society". But there are certain sacrifices involved and certain reservations one will have to reflect upon despite the development and advancement in all major aspects of the Khasi tribes.

It may be safely stated that, though Christianity has impacted considerably on the thoughts and beliefs of the Khasi tribes, leading to almost a blurring of their cultures, and despite the profound and unquestionable impact of Christianity, there are some rituals that have persisted and detached from Christian beliefs. It is very much apparent in the community that some of the indigenous beliefs are still adhered to and have not been mixed up with spiritual extensions. Hence, there can be instances of both conflict and negotiation.

The objective in taking up this topic for the chapter stems from the curiosity of finding out if there are conflicts or negotiations rather between the Khasis who belong to the indigenous faith and those who have converted and embraced other faiths including Christianity. Generations of Khasis are exposed through interactions and conversations both in the family and the community at large, with those belonging both to the indigenous belief and other faiths. It will indeed be interesting to study and examine the interface between the traditional beliefs and the transformation through conversion and of course the attempts at synthesizing the traditional practices and Christianity.

In matters related to birth, marriage and death, conflicts and negotiations occur to either be solved amicably or to also result in unpleasant encounters. Within one's own family there can be conflicting opinions and perspectives on these important practices. There was an instance in the family when on the death of a lady, whose children were partly Christian converts and partly followers of the indigenous traditional practices, there were conflicting arguments. The lady was neither a church attendee nor practiced the traditional rites and rituals. But when she died however, there was a misunderstanding.

The children belonging to the Christian faith wanted her to be buried while the others wanted her to be cremated. Furthermore, a few of her children wanted all the formalities of the traditional practices to be completed before she was carried out of the house, while the others wanted the reading of the *Bible* followed by a Christian prayer. In the end it was a compromise – a hybridized kind of a ceremony. The traditional rituals of breaking an egg and chanting by the priest were done. This was then followed by a reading from the *Bible* and a Christian prayer before the body was taken away to be buried and not cremated. Back from the cemetery, the Christian children wanted to clean up the house for the condolence prayer service. Those of the traditional faith wanted everything to be as it, till the third night, '*ka laitia*' was over. This incident resulted in an encounter and a conflict that appeared to be subtle but no doubt created a certain uncomfortable strain and unwanted rift among the family members.

Again, there are certain practices, even if not so significant, that often create differences in a family where members belong to two different belief systems. For instance, in death, after a body sponge, if it is a woman, the left side of the *jainsem* will have to cover the right and not in the usual manner of the right covering the left. This practice however creates a tension between the Christians and the Khasi indigenous believer as the Christians believe that this is no longer important.

Another example of an encounter in the family is the situation of an unnatural death. It is a common belief among the Khasis that those who die unnatural deaths will have to go through different rituals which includes the *'mait tyrut'* to ward off the so-called generational curse. Interestingly there is a divided opinion among the Khasis where this is concerned. Most Khasi Christians do not consider this important anymore since they affirm that their faith with prayer has cleansed away any kind of curse. They believe that spiritual armours defeat culturally biased superstitions. Again, in such nature of deaths, the deceased is not usually kept indoors but kept outside in a specially prepared enclosure. This is strongly practiced by the Khasis following the indigenous faith, but again most Christians follow this practice. However, this can create an unnecessary encounter and sometimes an unpleasant misunderstanding between the families since those who are more orthodox in their Christian beliefs ignore this as not significant anymore.

In the indigenous belief, a woman in the family way is advised not to visit a cremation site or visit the house where an unnatural death had taken place. This is emphasized strictly by the indigenous believers but though many Christian converts do not adhere to this practice, some families still do.

Again, in most Christian houses where a death has occurred, the placing of food both mornings and evenings and a lighted candle or lamp beside the deathbed till the body is carried for its burial are very much indigenous practices, but are practiced in some Christian homes.

Further, '*u kwai u tympew*' which is distributed to all funeral attendees on reaching the crematorium is an important indigenous practice. The same is done even among Khasi Christian converts though with a difference, since in the indigenous practice, the betel nuts are not cleaned but cut into pieces and the betel leaves are not smeared with lime. The practice of leaving all doors and windows unbarred till after the third night and the night watch called '*ka laitia*', for three consecutive nights, since it is believed that the spirit of the dead is still in the house is again practiced not only among those of the indigenous faith but even in some Christian homes.

In relation to marriages, beginning with the engagement, there are practices followed by those of the indigenous faith which are incorporated in the Christian ceremonies while some can raise conflicting perspectives within a family. To cite an instance in the family, in the engagement ceremony of a male member of the family, members of the woman's family invited the mother of the groom to be present for the engagement dinner though according to traditional beliefs, the mother or any female member are strictly exempted from being part of the engagement ceremony. The visit of the to-be mother-in-law to the girl's house is absolute taboo since only the male members were to accompany the person. The elders in the boy's family therefore strongly resented the idea leading to an unpleasant misunderstanding between the family members who felt that the occasion was a matter of knowing both families.

The arrangement for the wedding was even more complicated since the younger members of the family wanted a combine reception, while the seniors insisted that the wedding be celebrated in separate venues since according to the traditional beliefs; the mother of the groom should not see the daughter-in-law on the wedding day. A subtle conflict was very much inherent between not only the senior and younger members of both the families but also between those who follow the indigenous faith and those who are Christian converts.

But there are also instances of negotiation in the rituals of marriage. In the morning, before the groom leaves his house to go to the bride's, the family of the bride sends a pot of white plain rice (*ja synlar*) and a pot of unsalted boiled pork (*doh jynlat*) to the groom's house. The groom will have to have a serving of this before he leaves his mother's house to meet his bride. This is practiced not only by believers of the indigenous faith, but by Christians as well.

Further, the smearing of the oil on the forehead of both the groom and the bride by the bride's mother, symbolic of a welcome to the family gesture to the bride's home is a traditional practice which is followed till date by Christian Khasis.

On the third day after the marriage, the groom takes his wife to his mother's house. The couple is accompanied by the female relatives of the bride. The bride takes with her gifts, fruits and most often '*u putharo'*, the rice cake, as a token of respect to her in-laws. This custom is followed by all Khasis alike, irrespective of their faith.

In relation to birth, there are certain beliefs that can create encounters between the two faiths. For example, during pregnancy, the father is forbidden to hunt, complete the weaving and plaiting of a basket or bamboo work, or fire a piece of red-hot iron, or use it as such actions are believed to adversely affect the health of the child (Mawrie 1981:74). This conflicts with the understanding of most Khasi Christians. Interestingly however, some Christians still observe these practices which have been handed down over generations.

These are some of the events which have set one to think and reflect upon the efforts of the Christian church in proselytizing because the indigenous practices still continue to manifest in many situations. Though a number of studies have been done on the impact of traditional cultural practices on the Christian religion among the Khasis, there is still further scope for study to find out if there are possible cultural encounters or negotiations between Christianity that is being practised locally and the indigenous practices.

One can say that "Despite the real differences and even disparities between culture and religions, there is a basic stratum of human commonalities that can make it possible for people to communicate with one another and to discover points of contact with others" (Gort,

2008 : 756). Culture is intertwined with the religious aspect and beliefs of the Khasi people. So much so, it becomes very complicated for the present generation to clearly understand their own stance on their own identity, which led them to search for answers from the past and their history. It becomes more intriguing for researchers, intellectuals, folklorists, archaeologists and historians in dealing with this topic. Today, the Khasi society is like a melting pot where outside cultures co-exist with the Khasi culture. It's interesting and also challenging to analyse, as we consider the effects of globalization as it is at times becomes a process of 'homogenization' by which the world becomes increasingly uniform.

Richard Barnet and John Cavanagh write that the global shopping mall is a planetary supermarket with a dazzling spread of things to eat, drink, wear, and enjoy. Dreams of affluent living are communicated to the farthest reaches of the globe, but only a minority of the people in the world can afford to shop at the mall. Of the 5.4 billion people on earth, almost 3.6 billion have neither cash nor credit to buy much of anything. A majority of people on the planet are at most window–shoppers' (Cavanagh and Barnet, 1995:15). A new discourse will be needed to study the widespread development of globalization and its impact on culture and religion. Khasi indigenous religions have undergone rapid changes, where choral singers have also now become similar to the choir singers found in Christian services. Youths also participate zealously in their services in their modern-day attire and gadgets. Now, Christian religious services have also begun incorporating traditional music in their churches. Uncertainty is prevalent within Khasi society, but in spite of it, this will open new doors to a world of opportunities for researchers and scholars. Especially, in aligning and studying the unknown and untouched areas, which will ultimately be led to further understanding on a new venture. One can take up folklore, by unearthing the lost oral narratives in joining the coerced puzzle that has left many people to question their notion of identity which has helped to strengthen some while others have been plunged into crisis. But, if one takes up folklore, theoretical approaches such as the Motif- Index of Folk Literature, psycho-analytic theory, Levi Strauss's theory of structuralism and others are sure to provide valuable insights to these questions of identity. It is believed that by analysing folklore, one may potentially discover the patterns of culture which may lead to knowledge which may then provide the means of raising conscious awareness of one's identity. Ultimately, this may lead to a better understanding of the nuances of the Khasi worldview and how the Khasis looked at the world before the influence of these outside forces that have impacted its cultural space as well as its way of life. Snaitang aptly states, "The introduction of an inclusive religion did not undermine the traditional social structure or polity. It rather served as a means of bringing together the fragmented parts of the society into a new whole, under the auspices of a new ideology" (Snaitang, 1993: 161). One can delve deeper into this narrative to define, describe and explain conversion and conviction in the backdrop of the present social setting.

REFERENCES

Bareh, Hamlet. (1985). *The History and Culture of the Khasi People.* Guwahati: Spectrum Publications.

Cavanagh, J. & Barnet, Richard. J. (1995). *Global Dreams: Imperial Corporation and the New World Order.* New York: Simon and Schuster.

Gort, J.D. (2008). The Search for Interreligious Connivance, Ongoing Challenge and Charge. *Verbum et Ecclesia, 29*(3), 744-763.

Jyrwa, J.F. (2011). *Christianity in Khasi Culture.* Shillong: M.B. Jyrwa.

Mawrie, H.O. (1981). *The Khasi Milieu.* New Delhi: Concept Publishing Company.

Snaitang, O.L. (1993). *Christianity and Social Change in North East India.* Shillong: Vendrame Institute.

Syiemlieh, M. (2013). Early Response to Christian Missions: Challenges, Acceptance and Assertion in *Journal of Humanities and Social Science, 14*(2), 36-43.

11
Rumours, Suspicions, and the Making of the Narrative

Remembering the *Secret Killings* in Assam

Dixita Deka

Secret Killings in Assam: An Introduction

Assam has witnessed extraordinary events of violence arising out of people's movements, armed struggles, and ethnic conflicts. While the intensity of violence is measured based on the official statistics of casualties, the trauma of these events continues to haunt human lives and shape their identities, if not healed. The Assam Movement of 1979 that brought people across the state together against the illegal immigration from Bangladesh has also been the catalyst in triggering many other small-scale or long-term political upheavals in the region. The one with the gravest outcomes has been the armed struggle of the insurgent organization, United Liberation Front of Asom (ULFA) that found a platform to grow in the Assam Movement.

ULFA was formed on 7 April, 1979 at Rangghar in Sivasagar with its central theses that India has illegally occupied Assam and the Central Government has politically and economically exploited the resource rich region. The movement for a sovereign Assam involved many phases from popular support to public backlash, from state suppression to its revival, from internal schisms to peace talks, yet continuing to make its presence felt in the bordering regions of Assam. Most of these transitions involved stories of despair, loss, and mourning particularly for the civilians. This chapter is an attempt to remember one such event that has occurred during the counter-insurgency operations in Assam in the late 1990s. Those were the secret killings, popularly referred to as *gupto hoitya* that has never been acknowledged by the then state government of Assam.

Secret killings in Assam involved the torture, death, and subsequent disappearance of the relatives, close aides, and suspected sympathizers of ULFA by 'masked men' or 'unidentified assailants'. These killings occurred between 1998 and 2001 with two popular intentions: one, compelling the family members to persuade their underground kin to surrender, and two, creating a fear psychosis in the society preventing the people from supporting and sheltering insurgents. Over 300 people were killed but no one has been convicted in the secret killings in Assam and the families continue to live without legal and emotional closure. These events of extreme violence and grief have remained off the national gaze and add to the chapters of extra-judicial executions in Northeast India.

On November 28, 1990, the Central Government had imposed the President's Rule in Assam and declared the state a 'disturbed region'. On the next day, Operation Bajrang was declared under the leadership of Lieutenant General K.S. Brar. The army succeeded in arresting ULFA cadres from Upper Assam, and many underground camps were busted. The army was allegedly accused of harassment and gang-rape of young girls and women in the villages during the operation (Talukdar & Kalita, 2011, p. 207). They recovered mass graves from the infamous and abandoned ULFA camps at Lokhipothar, and the region came under the strict surveillance of the armed forces. Journalists, intellectuals, and human rights activists were soon booked under the National Security Act (NSA).

During this time, the leadership in ULFA refused to compromise their demand for sovereignty. They retaliated against the army by unleashing equal terror through killings, abductions, and creating instability in state governance. As a result, Operation Rhino began in 1991 to counter the violent activities of the insurgent organization. Detentions continued under the Terrorist and Disruptive Activities Act (TADA). The arrests or the surrender of cadres who held vital positions in ULFA succeeded in bringing the initial ruptures within the outfit that shaped the politics of counter-insurgency in Assam after that.

While the killing of journalist Parag Kumar Das in Guwahati on 17 May, 1996 was remembered by some of my informants as the beginning of the secret killings, others have considered the killing of ULFA

Chairman, Arabinda Rajkhowa's elder brother, Dimba Rajkonwar in 1998 to be the first secret killing in Assam. However, conversations with the family members and close aides of the deceased have strongly indicated the political face of those executions, and they refrained from remembering these as 'secret' when their traumatic experiences under counter-insurgency readily suspect the security forces that had attempted to criminalize their everyday lives.

So far, the secret killings have been narrated in fiction, as a sub-section or footnote to academic pieces on counter-insurgency, or in the official archives. This comfort of narrating the brutality and the painful experiences in fiction is corollary to the loss of vocabulary as described by Ruth Wajnryb (2001) on the Holocaust or the political significance behind such inexpressibility as explained by Elaine Scarry (1985). I intend to challenge the bureaucratic representation of the killings rooted in the victim-perpetrator binary, and shall try to articulate the need to look into the meta-data like rumours, silence, or denials as referred by Lee Ann Fujii (2010) in her work on the Rwandan genocide. Rumours and suspicions around the secret killings have not just informed official archives due to the fear and grief involved, but continue to shape people's narratives in remembering those killings in present times. Both in fiction, old and emerging, as well as my fieldwork across Assam, reflect the significance of rumours and suspicions in initiating these conversations.

How do people narrate?

Human memory is manipulative. It can shape the way certain events are looked at with ease, while others are avoided and overlooked. However, if such activities involve death, talking becomes uneasy. To understand how death shapes human life, it is imperative to discern the nature of such deaths. The focus then shifts from talking to telling or narrating events that people recognize, remember, or refuse to recall.

Defining secret killings is not difficult if one version of the narrative is taken into consideration, i.e., the official version. Secret killings in Assam were first acknowledged in 1998 when a dismembered leg of an adult human was found by two journalists on a dead stream in the village of Hudumpur at the outskirts of Guwahati (Talukdar, Borpujari & Deka, 2008). The two journalists, one of them being a photo journalist, were from the national daily *The Telegraph* and were on an assignment to verify if any mysterious killings were taking place on an embankment at Hudumpur near Palasbari on the bank of the river Brahmaputra. To their utter surprise, they broke the story of the secret killings for the first time and clicked the picture of the severed leg that became the cover image of the incident in press and literature. On further exploration, a villager had confessed to them of the regular recovery of human body parts in the area (Talukdar, Borpujari & Deka, 2008, p. 27):

The series of killings, preceding this revelation and after, marked the beginning of what the newspapers in Assam declared to be 'secret killings', owing to the mystery of the veiled killers. This mysterious nature made it difficult for anyone to define the secret killings until Justice K.N. Saikia Commission was constituted. The commission states that, "a killing may be secret as to the act of killing and/or as to the identity of the killers and/or as to the time or place of killing" (Justice K.N. Saikia Commission of Inquiry, 2006, p. 2). Comparing the killings with genocide where an entire race is wiped out, the commission emphasized on the deliberate killing of the ULFAs and their kiths and kin as ulfocide (Justice K.N. Saikia Commission of Inquiry, 2006, p.18). These were also referred to as the extra-judicial or extra-constitutional killings (Justice K.N. Saikia Commission of Inquiry, 2006, p. 37).

According to former Indian Police Service (IPS) officer Hiranya Kumar Bhattacharyya (2015), there were two intentions behind the secret killings: to pressurize the relatives of ULFA leaders and cadres to desist from their unlawful activities and, to create a fear psychosis amongst the public preventing them from sheltering ULFA cadres. The fact that the secret killings could neither draw mass surrenders post-1998 when the violence was extreme nor break people's empathy towards the victimized families of the insurgents and instead attracted strong protests, necessitates deeper engagement with the rationale behind the nature of counter-insurgency operations. The extra-judicial nature of such killings makes the conversations uneasy and intimidating. In this sense, the comfort of narrating the secret killings through fiction cannot be overlooked.

Citing Aruni Kashyap's (2013) novel, *The House with a Thousand Stories* and Arupa Patangia Kalita's (2001) novella, *Arunimar Swades* (Arunima's Own Country), Amit R. Baishya reflects upon the fictional representation of fear, suspicion, and rumours in the backdrop of the secret killings. According to him, these two texts signify the period of the secret killings not as an exception but a form of rule (Baishya, 2014). *Arunimar Swades* is based on the murder of Umakanta Gogoi and his family members at Sivasagar (Deka, 2019). Here, the author Arupa Patangia Kalita writes about the secret killers as *sayamurti manuh* (shadow men) and describes how Arunima's in-laws were under the surveillance of surrendered and unidentified gunmen, as one of her brothers-in-law was in the underground organization. During my fieldwork, one of my participants Barsha introduced me to the sensational secret killing of Umakanta Gogoi and his family. She narrated how there were news circulating around the village that three families: Umakanta Gogoi's family, one of their neighbour's, and that of her own, were under the radar of the secret killers and any possible attack on them could not be ruled out. However, even Barsha could not recall what the source of such information was. She just 'heard'.

Until 1999, when students' leader Ananta Kalita survived the attack by the secret killers and exposed the nexus between the surrendered cadres (SULFA), police and army behind the killings, there was a blanket denial. Even though people across Assam had witnessed the atrocities and the extra-judicial powers of the police and the SULFA, fear shaped confessions and conversations. It was in this context that, fiction continues to remain a comfortable and courageous medium in revisiting the past.

Kaushik Barua's (2020) short story, *Run to the Valley* situated in an urban setting, further builds upon the precarity of human lives under the counter-insurgency operations. Barua's story reflects upon a 'disturbed' Assam of the 1990s when the surrendered cadres enjoyed unchecked powers like retaining guns and acting as the local goons, and the police and the armed forces were given a freehand in maintaining 'law and order', thereby, staging anyone as a militant, arresting on suspicion, or killing anyone who was apparently a rebel in the eyes of the state. Such an image of the security personnel and the surrendered cadres has rendered them the tag of a traitor in remembering the secret killers.

Of rumours, Suspicions, and Traitors

There is a deep and intricate connection between rumours and suspicions. While researching on the politics of remembering the secret killings, I encountered with my participants' suspicions regarding my purpose of engaging with the forgotten event and my own suspicion of who was speaking the truth or what to expect from the interviews that did not follow a structured pattern. These suspicions have been the product of the abandoned and failed attempts at convicting the secret killers. At moments of lies, disloyalty, half-truths or ignorance, suspicions turn compelling, if not factual. The dissemination of these suspicious assumptions in the society regarding who could be the secret killers, what have been the reasons behind targeting someone, or what had made someone interested in studying the secret killings twenty years later turns into rumours which regenerate new information.

It is not an unknown human experience that bloody fights, wars, persecutions, and any other acts that are violent, painful, and traumatic, are inexpressible that recalling or narrating becomes impossible. Most of the rumours originate under such situations where there is a shortage of information or inability to reach out to those directly affected. In these moments, as Anna Simons (1995, p. 54) argues, "the third-person plural, the mysterious (numerous) 'they'" voice out the allegedly untarnished information. With evidentiary claims like 'I have heard', 'My trusted associates had told', most of the painful memories of human lives are recalled and narrated. Maintaining one's anonymity intact, often people try to present the truths as rumours to overcome the sense of guilt associated with silence and at the same time to conceal one's identity in fear of dreadful consequences. During my fieldwork, I came across many of such instances where the people I met expressed the need to revisit the secret killings and seemed to have intentionally left me with the names of people, my prospective participants whom 'they heard' possibly by the 'mysterious they', whom I should meet and who could offer me with helpful insights. The curiosity in my mind regarding the reasons how I could be recommended those names that had firsthand experience of witnessing or experiencing violence and its aftermath, constructed new assumptions. Self-reflexivity was omnipresent in the sense whether I should brush away these curiosities, accept it as it was, or be suspicious of it. In my interest, suspicions lay a network of assumptions, which if revealed without factual verification, could turn into rumours. This search for the possible causes behind rumours thus produces more rumours (Simons, 1995, p. 55). In societies under counter-insurgency operations, rumours such as these could often put the veil of suspicion on anyone: civilians, insurgents, or counter-insurgents.

At a time when people intentionally presented truths as rumours, there are also instances where rumours were traded as truths. To elaborate, rumours have been one of the mobilizing forces behind many acts of violence locally as well as globally. For instance, in explaining the peasants' uprising, Ranajit Guha (1983, p. 256) considers rumours to be the "natural and indispensable vehicle of insurgency". Speculations are raw when information could not be reached. Simons further considers this tendency to '"educe, collapse, and edit out the very terror of not-knowing" at the genesis of rumours (Simons, 1995, p. 55). Veena Das has also re-emphasized on the "anonymity of the source of rumour, its capacity to build solidarity, and the overwhelming urge it prompts in listeners to pass it on to others" (Das, 1998, p. 116) that characterize rumours building her argument on Guha's analysis. Later in her work, she has illustrated how rumours emerge and periodically re-emerge under political disturbances where people live under the spell of suspicion against each other from the same group, against the 'other', as well as the government that has failed to offer one a sense of security and dignified life. She cites the example of India's former Prime Minister Indira Gandhi who was speculated to be assassinated even before her death for avenging the counter-insurgency operation at the Golden Temple in Amritsar, code named Operation Blue Star in July 1984 and rumours had made its rounds on the possible identity of her assassins even before any official announcement (Das, 1998, p. 110). Based on the perspective from which an act of violence or a traumatic event is remembered, the images are reversed, that of a perpetrator and a victim (Das, 1998, p. 111). This offers an opportunity to reinforce the assumed stories of one's mind as truths with incomplete information or in its absence. Rumours tend to generalize and turn communication infectious thereby employing sweeping vocabulary (Pandey, 2001, p. 68). Any further attempt to disseminate these assumptions or half-truths for clarification helps towards its circulation, which at times produces grave outcomes.

In the absence of any evidence or legal acknowledgment, rumours continue to circulate even today who the secret killers were or who had offered them the logistical support in carrying out the ghastly murders in Assam. Gossips connected to the background of the families who were targeted also continue to add to the narrative, at times mourning those deaths reclaiming their innocence and at the other times justifying the 'logical reasons' behind these killings given their association with the underground organization was concerned. In her seminal work, *Rumour, Rhetoric, Rebellion: Negotiating the archive and the witness in Assam,* Rakhee Kalita Moral (2015) explains the significance of rumours in understanding the social dynamics of insurgency.

In the backdrop of mid-eighties and early nineties when ULFA had started making its presence in the society with its activism, recruitment drives, as well as then rumoured linkages with other insurgent groups for armed training, Moral (2015, pp.11-12) emphasized how local gossips found its space in the way people's allegiance to the insurgent movement was navigated. She highlighted how gossips connected to who joined ULFA or who served as overground sympathizers helped in identifying the allies, aides, or associates of the insurgent organization (Moral, 2015, p.12). Rumours connecting to one's categorical identification such as this overlook one's individuality and individual choices, and often provides them with the label of a traitor. In most of such violent settings, it does not take long for the rumours to turn the erstwhile traitors as the targets to be penalised. Anuradha Sharma Pujari's (2020) short story *Surrender* navigates the life of one such surrendered cadre, Dipok, who had once joined the underground organization to bring about revolution, and ended up being suspected by the policemen, his neighbours and even his wife. Eventually, Dipok's surrendered life not just left him frustrated but also failed to free him from the past, of its curses and taunts, and of the surveillance. The story ends with Dipok's killing by 'unknown assassins' when he had informed the police of his former fellow comrades involved in the killing of two military officers. The crux of the story lays on the burden of being a surrendered cadre even in their overground lives.

Understanding the secret killings in Assam, and more so remembering it, is complicated because of the kind of intimate connections the insurgents shared with the civilians then, and/or with their comrades who later surrendered. The fear or the guilt of betrayal prevented my participants across their categorical identities to speak about their alleged intimacy with the insurgents or the state thereby sharing the mysterious third-person narratives or subsequent denials without further explanation. Researching the secret killings around twenty years later, I witnessed how the affected families have expanded the definitive scope of traitors to cover not just the state, the police, and the surrendered insurgents who were allegedly involved in the killings directly, but also their neighbours in some cases, and ULFA itself, in most of the cases. Their change in perception from being the supporters of the insurgent struggle to being indifferent to the underground leadership was rooted both in their grudge and pain of leading tough lives, mostly without legal or emotional closure. The extreme fear of getting one's trust broken again, suspicions persist in the way my participants continuously read and observed me.

The availability of the digital reports helped me not just in reading about the cases, but mostly in getting rough ideas to geographically locate the forgotten families. Even in exploring the significance of documents like these, I readily observed people's memories attached not just to the 'official' tag of these documents, but for many, these documents bear the evidence of the ordeal they had to undergo in the past or as the last piece of memento of their loved ones. Almost at every house, I visited to meet the families of victims or the survivors, my respondents had shown me neatly kept copies of official documents, handwritten complaints, photographs, newspaper cuttings, and newsletters connected to their stories. Mapping through memories based on both testimonies and other sources offer a nuanced understanding of violence that at times, is unspeakable and breaks through the homogenous or categorical lens to recall rumours, realities, or revelations.

When the Evidence is Not Enough: Concluding Thoughts

Justice K.N. Saikia Commission, a one-person commission, was appointed in 2005 by the then incumbent Congress in Assam led by Chief Minister Tarun Gogoi to investigate into the killings. It is imperative to note here that Congress came into power in Assam in 2001 defeating the regional political party Asom Gana Parishad (AGP) having kept the investigation into the secret killings as one of its central agendas of electoral manifesto. Justice K.N. Saikia Commission was preceded by three other commissions: Justice Shafiqul Haque Commission, Justice Meera Sarma Commission, and Justice J.N. Sharma Commission. The first commission was appointed to investigate into the sensational abduction and attempt to murder of student leader Ananta Kalita from Hajo in Kamrup district (Deka, 2021a). Despite his upfront confessions and testimonials on the involvement of the police-SULFA-army nexus, Kalita's case was never resolved. In the second commission, Justice Meera Sarma is said to have resigned citing non-cooperation from the police (Talukdar, Borpujari & Deka, 2008, p. 8). In 2003, Justice J.N. Sharma Commission was formed but yet again failed to convict anyone (Talukdar, Borpujari & Deka, 2008, p. 9).

In 2007, Saikia Commission published four reports covering 35 cases where the commission had claimed that the "then Home Minister was at the helm of these extra-Constitutional killings" (Government of Assam, Department of Home and Political, 2007). This was further reiterated in my conversations with the families of the victims who had registered scorn against the then government in its unwillingness to address the gross grievances of the families. However, what was striking for me to hear was the reluctance of many families to register police cases at the abduction, disappearance or killing of their family members due to the urgency of keeping the other members safe. The secret killings tend to establish an extreme sense of fear where people refrained from fighting the cases legally. Families were broken and the members were in a constant run for their life. Even when the government began compensating a few families as recommended by the commission, many families ceased to come forward to claim the money. As drawn from people's memories, it was the human rights organization Manab Adhikaar Sangram Ṣamiti (MASS) that assisted them to courts (Deka, 2021b). However, what makes a conversation on the secret killings long due is the recent development of the Saikia Commission being quashed by the Gauhati High Court in September 2018 (*The Assam Tribune*, 2018). Remembering the secret killings seemed to be analogous to many such violent memories of counter-insurgency that transcend the spatial boundaries of the region. In North-east India alone, civilians have often fallen into the tussle between the insurgents and the counter-insurgents. At a time when evidence is not enough, it becomes essential to go back to the different manifestations of memories that have the potential to revisit the forgotten stories of violence from conflict zones. In this regard, a conversation on the suspicions and rumours over the ultimate search for truth may be a good place to start with.

REFERENCES

Baishya. A.R. (2014, March). The 'secret killings' of Assam in literature. *Himal Southasian*. https://www.himalmag.com/secret-killings-of-assam-in-literature/

Bhattacharyya, H.K. (2015). *Betrayal of North East: The Arrested Voice*. Manas Publications.

Barua, K. (2020). Run to the Valley. In Aruni Kashyap (Ed.), *How to tell the Story of an Insurgency: Fifteen Tales from Assam* (pp.130-141). Harper Collins Publishers.

Das, V. (1998). Specificities: Official Narratives, Rumour, and the Social Production of Hate. *Social Identities Journal for the Study of Race, Nation and Culture*, *4*(1), 109-130. https://www.tandfonline.com/doi/abs/10.1080/13504639851915.

Deka, D. (2019, March). Who remembers the secret killings in Assam. *Raiot*. http://www.raiot.in/who-remembers-the-secret-killings-in-assam/

Deka, D. (2021a). Living without closure: memories of counter-insurgency and secret killings in Assam. *Asian Ethnicity*, *22*(3),428-446. https://doi.org/10.1080/14631369.2019.1639492

Deka, D. (2021b). *Suppressed silences: women as witnesses and the wounds of witnessing secret killings in Assam*. Zubaan Publishers Pvt. Ltd.

Fujii, L.A. (2010). Interpreting truth and lies in stories of conflict and violence. In C. Lekha Sriram, J.C. King, J.A. Mertus, O.Martin-Ortega & J.Herman (Eds.), *Surviving Field Research: Working in violent and difficult situations* (pp.147-162). Routledge.

Government of Assam, Department of Home and Political. (2007). *Action Taken Report on the Report Submitted by Justice (Retd) K.N. Saikia Commission of Inquiry*. Department of Home and Political, Government of Assam.

Guha, R. (1983). *Elementary Aspects of Peasant Insurgency in Colonial India*. Oxford University Press.

Justice K.N. Saikia Commission of Inquiry. (2006). *Report of Justice K.N. Saikia Commission of Inquiry on the first group of seven cases on Secret Killings*. Justice K.N. Saikia Commission of Inquiry.

Kashyap, A. (2013). *The House with a Thousand Stories*. Penguin Books, India.

Moral, R.K. (2015). *Rumours, Rhetoric, Rebellion: Negotiating the archive and the witness in Assam*. Nehru Memorial Museum and Library.

Pandey, G. (2001). *Remembering Partition: Violence, Nationalism and History in India*. Cambridge University Press.

Patangia, A.K. (2001). *Arunimar Swadesh (Arunima's Country)*. Jyoti Prakashan.

Pujari. A.S. (2020). Surrender. In Aruni Kashyap (Ed.), *How to tell the Story of an Insurgency: Fifteen Tales from Assam* (pp.1-14). Harper Collins Publishers.

Scarry, E. (1985). *The Body in Pain: The Making and the Unmaking of the World.* Oxford University Press.

Simons, A. (1995). The Beginning of the End. In C.Nordstrom & A.C.G.M. Robben (Eds.), *Fieldwork under fire: contemporary studies of violence and survival* (pp. 42-59). University of California Press.

Talukdar, M., Borpujari, U. & Deka, K. (2008). *Secret Killings of Assam: The Horrific story of Assam's darkest period.* Nanda Talukdar Foundation and Bhabani Books.

Talukdar, M., & Kalita, K.K. (2011). *ULFA*. Nanda Talukdar Foundation.

The Assam Tribune. (2018, September 4). HC Quashes K.N. Saikia Report on Secret Killings. *The Assam Tribune*.

Wajnryb, R. (2001). *The Silence: how tragedy shapes talk.* Allen & Unwin.

Index

Agriculture and livelihood activities, impact of ethnic conflict on, 105
Alienation and Existentialism in relation to Literature and Youth, 39
All-Party Central Language Action Committee, 24
Anti-homosexuality laws, 62, 63
Anti-Tamil pogrom, 3
Arunimar Swades, 140, 141
Asian community, 74
AsianBoss, 75
Assam Maintenance of Public Order (Autonomous Districts) Act, 1953, 118
Assam, 103

Bangladesh,
  identity-related politics and intermittent violence in the last four decades, 27
  lessons learnt or being learnt in from identity-related conflicts and violence, 30
Baptist Missionaries of Serampore, 128
Beauty, 76, 77, 81
  colourist perception of, 77
  industry, 77
Bengal, first partition of and questions of identity till partition (1905-1947), 19
Bengali immigration, 103
Bible, 65
Biopolitics, 38
Biopower, 36
Bodoland Territorial Area District (BTAD) in Assam,
  background of ethnic conflict in, 104
  impact of ethnic conflict on agriculture and sustainable rural development in, 102-110
Bodoland Territorial Council (BTC), 104
Bodos, 103,105
Boro Binyakhata village, 108
Brave New World, 30
Building Peace: Sustainable Reconciliation in Divided Societies, 121

Catholic Imagination, 60, 63
Cease Fire Agreement, 119
Charter Act of 1813,128
Christianity, 65, 114, 127, 131
Citizenship Act of 1948, 7
Colonialism and colourism, 73
Conflict, xi, 33, 47,
  environmental change, dwindling resources and their relationship with, 88
  in Syria, 91
  inevitability of, 92

the Naga story of, 113-126
Constitution of India, 129
Crossing Borders, 54
Cultural boundaries, 127
Curriculum Vitae, 66, 69

Dark Skin, curing—the psychological trauma of darkness, 78
Dark skinned Filipinas,77
Dayton Peace Agreement, 55
Deeply divided societies, 122, 123
anatomy of, 121
Nagas—a typical case of, 123
Diasporic Sri Lankan writing, 9
Divide and rule policy, 20
Dreams of affluent living, 135

East and South-east Asia, culture of, 75
East Pakistan, identity related politics and violence in (1947-1971), 23
Eastern Bengal and Assam, 20
Ekushey February, 24
Environmental change, 87
Environmental issues, 90
Establishment nationalism, 25
Ethnic group, 102

Factionalism, 124
Federal Government of Nagaland (FGN), 118, 120
Femininity, 49
Financial resources, 98
First World, 5, 6
Freudian concept of trauma, 42

Gender and conflict, 47-58
Gender mainstreaming, 49
Gender violence, 48
Global Ideal Asian/Filipina Beauty, 74
Government of India Act, 1935, 115
Greenhouse gases (GHGs), 87

Half-widows, 51
Hindu-Muslim tensions, 17
Homo Sacer, 37
Human memory, 139
Hydari Agreement, 116

Identity and Violence: The Illusion of Destiny, 18, 21
Illegal migration, 94
Indian Statutory Commission, 114

Janatha Vimukthi Peramuna (JVP), 3, 4
Justice K.N. Saikia Commission, 145
Justice Shafiqul Haque Commission, 145
JVP uprising, 8, 9

Kashmiri society, 50
Khasi Christians, 129
Khasi diaspora, 129
Khasi Hills, 128
Khasi indigenous beliefs and Christianity, 127-136

Liberation Tigers of Tamil Elam (or the LTTE), 4, 7, 11, 13

Mad Woman in the Attic, 59
Manab Adhikaar Sangram Samiti (MASS), 146
Masculinity, 49
Migrant-host dynamics, 92
Migration, 91
across borders in Asia, 94
does environmental change lead to, 90
Muslim League, 21

Naga Club, 115
Naga conflict, 113
Naga Hills District Tribal Council, 115

Naga identity, 113
Naga national consciousness, 114
Naga National Council (NNC), 115, 116, 117
Naga nationalist movement, 114
Naga People's Convention' (NPC), 119
Nagaland Baptist Church Council (NBCC), 119
Nagas, 113
National identity formation, confronting violence relating to (a Bangladeshi perspective), 15-32
National Socialist Council of Nagaland (NSCN), 120
Native *morena* identity, 80
Natural resources, 89
Naya Kashmir Manifesto, 56
Nazi state, 36
New Testament, 15
Northeast India, 113, 114

Obsession with beauty, 76
Orientalism, 4

Pan-Naga nationalistic project,114
Patriarchy, 48
People's Sovereign Republic of Free Nagaland, 117
Philippines, 73, 74
  mental health and self-esteem of women in, 80
Political landscape of a nation, 89
Politics of colour, 80
Population growth, 88
Post-colonial nationalism, 11
Post--traumatic stress, 55
Post-war reconstruction, 52
Pro-immigration policies, 94

Queer people, 66
Queer, 65

Racism, 36
Resources, accessibility and availability of, 97
Responsibility to be beautiful—why fairness matters, 76
Rohingya poetry, 43
Rohingyas, imagery and reality—art from the, 33-44
Rumour, Rhetoric, Rebellion: Negotiating the archive and the witness in Assam, 144
Run to the Valley, 141

Saikia Commission, 146
Secret Killings in Assam, rumours, suspicions, and the making of the narrative, 137
Sergius Seeks Bacchus, 59, 61, 62, 63
  re-imagining the Catholic Imagination—queer, self and conflict in Norman E. Pasaribu's, 59-72
Shillong Accord, 1975, 120
Simon Commission Memorandum, 115
Sinhala creative writing, 7
Sinhala literature, 7
Skin colour hierarchy, 79
  the ideal Filipina beauty and the conflict of colour, 73-84
Social patriarchy, 47
South-Southeast Asia,
  a study of the relationship between environmental change, migration and conflict: 87-101
  conflict facilitating factors, 94
    ethnic, religious and cultural divides, 95
    land use, resource access and employment, 96
    the political milieu, 94
Speaking Peace: Women's Voices from Kashmir, 55

Sri Lankan civil life, 3
Sri Lankan creative writing in English, 8
Sri Lankan writing and terror, 6
State racism, 35
SULFA, 141
Swadeshi movement, 20

Taliban, 52
Terror,
  affect and literary representation—reflections on Sri Lankan writing in a South Asian frame, 3-14
  representing terror in a global era of terror, 12
  the nation state and the post-colony, 4
  the subjective experience of, 3
Terrorist and Disruptive Activities Act (TADA), 138
Thai Government, 96
The Armed Forces (Special Powers) Act, 1958 (AFSPA), 118
The Assam Disturbed Areas Act, 1955, 118
The History and Culture of the Khasi People, 128
The House with a Thousand Stories, 140
The Merchant of Venice, 15, 16
The Mirror Stage as Formative of the function of the I as Revealed in Psychoanalytic Experience, 40
The World and the Home, 34
Third World, 6, 10, 11
This Was Not Our War, 54
Trauma, 'historical power' of the, 42
Treaty of Yandabo of 1826, 124

U Dohlieh, 131
Unfinished Memoirs, 21, 22
United Liberation Front of Asom (ULFA), 6, 137, 138,140, 144, 145
United Nations Organisation (UNO), 123
Unmaking Home, 34

Welsh Presbyterian mission, 128
Widows, 51
Women,
  in conflict situations, 53
  sexual abuse and rape of, 56
Women's Action Forum (WAF), 56